A ROAD YOU MUST TRAVEL

First published by AuthorHouse
05/11/2010
Re-edited Version 2015
ISBN: 978-1 4520-2396-0 (e)
ISBN: 978-1 4520-2395-3 (sc)
ISBN: 978-1 4520-2394-6 (hc)
Library of Congress Control Number:
2010906692
Printed in the United States of America
Bloomington, Indiana: This book is printed on acid-free paper.

A ROAD YOU

MUST TRAVEL

I dedicate this book to all women and men looking for true love.
I dedicate this book to all women and men who have gone
through a struggle of any kind, whether it was a marriage, a bad
breakup, loss of a loved one, or even the loss of your home.

~ 7 ~

ACKNOWLEDGMENTS

First, I would like to thank my Lord and savior, Almighty God. Without Him this book would not be possible. He is my truth and the light, and I love Him so, words cannot express the way I feel. He has always been my Father, my first love and the light of my being.

I would like to thank my loving husband, Anthony Freeman, who has always supported me in whatever I wanted to do in life. He has allowed me to write about our deepest secrets, hurts and happiness. He has allowed me to let the world into our home. He has always been a close friend, the love of my life; he is my true soul mate. God has truly blessed me.

I thank my mother, Miriam, for instilling the faith of God in me and teaching me the value of responsibility because without that, I don't know where I would be right now.

Introduction

My life is normal, a life full of unexpected occurrences. I am a mother with three beautiful sons, along with my beloved husband, who supports me in my endeavors. The responsibilities that I carry as a wife and a mother can feel a little overwhelming. However, there's no doubt in my mind that this is the life I would choose all over again if I had a choice.

This book is truly my testimony. It is filled with painful memories and good memories. It contains inserts from my personal diaries. I speak the truth. The events and feelings that I chose to share are for your inspiration. I want you to know that you are not the only one who has gone through a horrible ordeal; I just hope it wasn't like mine.

The persons or person in this story you will read about are real characters, but because I respect them I have not used their real names. The story I tell you is true. I am just telling my side of the story. My story consists of years of emotional and spiritual battles, dealing with regret, deceit and trust, but most of all a search for true love. Love can be a strange but strong a word that we all seem to search for the true meaning.

We all pray that love finds us, or we may give up and look for it. You want to know the truth behind love and the experience from it, but what comes with it is a lot of work and patience.

Everyone deserves to experience true love, the kind of love that is patient, kind, and gives back when given; but never the kind of love that takes and takes and never gives in return. I am talking about emotional things, not physical things. Things can never amount to true love. In this book, you will read that I was a seeker and a giver. I gave my love and at one point, I didn't get love back in return. What I did get wasn't love at all.

I used my voice as a tool to get what I thought I deserved, but my voice was not heard and my love was not received.

I was shut off and pushed away. Something happened...But you will have to travel my road to find out.

I want you to remember as you take the journey back in my past that there are going to be some bumps and maybe even some hills. What I have in store for you will let you know that you won't be stuck in the valley too long. I will surely lead you through this journey very carefully, so if you get stuck just take a moment and give yourself some time. You will be able to come back on the ride and begin again. If I baffle you in any way, remember that I am no longer in this valley, but I am free because God delivered me. Remember, I wasn't alone on this journey that I share with you today. I have overcome and the best is yet to come. I am always looking forward, never to the left or the right, but up. Without the peace, joy and happiness that I have today, I wouldn't be where I am today, and that's being free.

In respect to God, without Him this book would not be possible, and without Him I would not be here today to tell my story. So, when I say, "Thank you God," I say THANK YOU GOD, with a loud voice and praise. Once you know where I've been, then you will know that, there is no God like my God, Jesus Christ. I hope you enjoy this book for it truly comes from the heart.

I hope I can bless you and give you something to take with you on your life's journey, for true love and happiness is a gift from God.

CHAPTER 1

A CRY FOR MY MOTHER

January 2, 2007

    Dear Diary,

I rose from my bed at one-thirty A.M. I felt like my mother has abandoned me; I felt like I needed my mom with me more than ever. Why am I feeling like this? These feelings of insecurity and loneliness are strange. It takes me back to a place in time when I couldn't have my mother next to me, holding me in her safe arms. As tears roll down my face, I see that lonely place, that place of darkness and fear. This is a place where no child needs to be; a place of loneliness. I cry out for my mother that's still here on Earth; a mother that's not far from me in miles, but seems as far as the stars. I need my mother so close to me now to share my thoughts, dreams, and happiness. I need the peace of mind knowing that my love is not being blocked. I need to know that I have her true friendship that was lost two years ago. Why do I need my mother so much when I have always depended on God? I'm not letting go of my faith, but there's a hunger inside of me for my mother that won't go away. There's a pain that can't be explained, not even to my husband. Lord, I need these answers that I feel only my mother has. Dreams and nightmares of anger and fights disturb me almost every night as I toss and turn uncontrollably, trying to find an answer to why I need my mother that's so dear to me. Our lives were so simple with happiness and laughter, but still surrounded with disappointments and pain. My mother and I seemed to pick each other up and ease fears to make them go away, even if it were for just a moment. We depended on each other to lift the other up. Through our hard struggles that we faced with our male relationships, we still managed to be there for each other. This need to connect with my mother is unexplainable, but I know I need to do so soon.

I paused to get more rest and the thoughts in my head just wouldn't go away. The sun has come up now and the clock says seven-fifty A.M. My mind kept thinking repeatedly, "Why did these feelings come about in the first place?" When I thought about it more and more, it came back to me.

It all began when I felt betrayed. Sometimes my feelings tell me that Mama raised us in the fear and admiration of God, but shielded her past and wrong doings as though she were perfect. She told me some things, but left much out. She told me the things I needed to hear to get me through whatever stage I was in, but seeing some things for myself as a child, I didn't pay much attention to them. Mama always taught us about being a kid and how the adults were the ones who made the decisions; so, I blocked out a lot. Now I see! Much of it has returned to my memory. I see now, I just turned my head and heart away so I wouldn't be affected by it.

I pretended as if nothing ever happened and if Mama was happy, so was I. I can remember how Mama always talked to me when

I felt strange about something or if she was having a dreadful day. I can remember her telling me to let God be the filler of the emptiness that I felt at eleven-years-old.

I longed to feel the love of a father, my father. The person that I could call "daddy" was a desire. I can remember having one for a brief period. My dad, (not blood, but as real as a dad could be) James Woods, was the first dad I came to know and the last stepfather I ever called daddy.

He called me "Tish Mo Nish," his favorite dish. I loved it when he called me such a name. I loved him with all my heart and I still miss him to this day. You see, he was a drunk by night and a step-father by day. That's how I remembered him.

My mother told me they were married eight years, but I only remember three of those years, age's four to six. Those years will always be with me. When I turned fourteen we received the news he passed away, still a drunk, hit by a passing truck.

I remember growing up on a little farm-like place called the country bliss; I considered it the best time of my life. My mother raised four of us, my two brothers, my sister and me.

We had an instant grandmother and grandfather James' parents. They were the best. They cooked fish, it seemed every day, leaving the heads of the fish on. As a child, I thought that wasn't the best idea. I can remember having cows and chickens in our backyard; they were off limits to us.

We had a well we played around. We ate the cactus fruit from the cactus; it reminded me of watermelon. I had the opportunity to watch my mother ring the chicken's neck. I stood on the side in amazement, watching the chickens continue to run around without heads. We also drank goat's milk straight from the goat, with our little cups in hand, waiting for seconds. Our neighbors owned horses instead of nice cars. Our roads were dirt instead of paved. I lived in the country, but little did I know, my country bliss would be short-lived.

Those were the days I felt life wasn't such a burden for my mother, but the truth remained, it was. My drunken stepfather became violent; for the stepfather, I knew was no longer a part of our lives. The money soon became little to none. I remember being told a cold bath was what we had to take because the electricity was off. I recall the water hose from outside being placed through the window from the neighbor's house giving us the water we needed. I faked being in the tub, by splashing the water, pretending I took a bath. We had no choice but to use candles to make light and borrow water to drink. Those days were just the beginning of our struggles. We moved from the countryside to more hills and struggles. My mother had to face life as a single mother of four. As I go back in time, I clearly see how much of my past I really tried to forget.

Even further in my past, when I was four, every day seemed like a struggle. Living on the West Coast was not our ideal place to be. We slept on the floor to avoid bullets that flew through our walls. We ate beans and rice almost every day for dinner because that's just what we had. We knew better than to play away from the eyes of our mother because guns were everywhere. The neighbors on our left and right made sure we knew that they didn't care how old we were, as they continued to flash their guns in the air. They shot them as if they were toy guns, shooting them in the air, then laughing to make them-selves known.

I feel myself remembering the nightmare of my past. The feelings start to come back in patches. It was a time in my life I struggled with for so long. It became a dark secret I didn't dare to tell. It was a dark, chilly night; I can remember as if it were yesterday. Three big bangs hit our front, hollow, wood door. Bang! Bang! Bang! My three older siblings and I all jumped up out of our sleep and ran to our mother's room. We thought a gang or some robbers had broken through the door.

As Mom looked out the window, she saw the bright lights of police cars and saw men holding huge flashlights in their hands. She opened the door, shocked and concerned. They flashed their lights in our kid faces. One officer said, "Ma'am we have reason to believe that you are neglecting your children."

You probably question how a four-year-old remembers such detail.

Never underestimate a child's ability to remember something so traumatizing.

She pleaded with the officer and cried as they led my crying older brothers, my sister and me away. I can remember trying to stay calm while calming my siblings by saying, "It's going to be alright, don't cry guys." As tears filled my eyes even now as I write; just writing this makes it hard for me to finish. "I must." I remember being pulled away from my mother as I clinched her legs tightly without crying. I kept thinking that I had to be strong for my mother and older siblings. I looked at my mother for assurance that everything would be okay. She then assured me, "It will be okay, and Mommy will come and get you all. It's ok."

I couldn't let them see me cry or I wouldn't be strong. We were taken to two complete strangers' houses, leaving us separated in two's. It was my brother and I closest in age, and my oldest brother and sister together. When we arrived at the house, the woman at the door was not very friendly, nor did she seem pleased that my brother and I were there. Time seemed to be endless and the days were longer than ever. She yelled to put us to bed and as soon as the lights went out, the tears flowed for the first time. I stared out of the window and looked up at the night sky as the moon shined in through the blinds. I prayed my mother would come get me. I was lost in a world and didn't know how to get home. I repeated my cry for my mother every night, from a loud cry, to a silent cry.

When we walked outside, I saw a neighborhood so clean and full of life, but deep down inside, it was the darkest place I had ever been. There were other kids living in the house also, and they seemed to have been there a good while because they knew the rules, and knew them well. Come to find out, my older brother and sister were having a ball, and my brother and I were getting the yelling and screaming. "Oh, my God, we were in foster care." My mother said we were gone for three weeks, but it felt like a lifetime.

Even though these were memories, I know them all too well. I had to deal with the pain and the hurt for so long, alone. My mother didn't know how to soothe the deep scary feelings I felt of being left alone. I had to call on God to help soothe the aches that I felt. I had to ask for God to help ease the pain that taunted me for years to come. My mother came and got us from that horrible place just like she had promised. As time went on living in this place became more and more dangerous.

The crime and the violence that threatened our lives every day became unbearable for my mother. My oldest brother was approaching the age of fifteen and as he became older he had to fight for his life every day to keep the gangs at bay.

I will never forget, one day as we walked in the doors from school, our mother tells us we are leaving. She keeps it simple by telling us to pack only what we could carry in a suitcase, for we would be leaving the same night. As we packed our things, we questioned her about where we would live. She simply stated, "We are moving to the Sunshine state to live with your Aunt, my sister." My brothers, sister and I had not known of any other place in the world other than the West Coast. This Sunshine state was like a foreign country. We still weren't prepared for the ride of our lives.

We ended up that same night at the Greyhound bus station to ride a bus for four days and three nights all the way to the beautiful state, which ended up being just that, sunny and bright.

January 2, 2007
Early in the Morning
Present Day

Dear Diary,

The feelings of being alone has crept up in my emotions; like long ago; it covered my body like a thick coat of darkness, yet it remains a question in my mind, "why do I feel this way at this very moment?" If we take a journey back in time two years ago when the end became the beginning for me and maybe for my mother, then you will know. It happened so suddenly, but time still was of the essence.

I was now a grown up, living in this beautiful state I call home. I had just left my husband of three years and high school sweetheart of six years. The years I was married to my high school sweetheart were so stressful and weighed down. They were filled with worries and lies.

My husband was a kid at heart and I chased after him like a hungry animal looking for love. All I found was lust. I loved him dearly, but defining the meaning of love at that time, was like trying to find a needle in a haystack.

I wanted so much to be loved by this man. I wanted to be cared for also. However, my husband did not do these things. I felt used. The love I gave did not return. While I kept the house clean and cooked countless meals, my husband was rarely around. He came home whenever he decided; food usually sat cold on the table. We were headed for divorce.

Our two kids, our boys, had no understanding of the divorce process. They did know that their mother loved them unconditionally. I very seldom cried in front of my kids. I did not want them to see the pain I had inside.

They had done nothing wrong; so, letting them endure such confusion was not an option. They were my God-given angels and I had to protect them.

While my husband remained in our home, I needed a place to stay. My sister opened her house to my two kids and me. Despite her problems, she was kind enough to take us in. She was nice enough to give us her daughter's bedroom, as her daughter was too young to complain about her lost space. Our children were okay; for all they knew, they could play with their cousins more regularly.

Although my kids were whom I mostly thought about, I pretended to have everything under control when it came to my emotions. However, God knew and so did my mother; I was torn inside. I was torn because I was without a place to call home, and bills were hanging over my head.

I had no money and no child support from my husband. Soon, feelings of loneliness came and knocked on my door, reminding me I was alone. I craved for love.

I still wanted love and I didn't even know it was right under my nose. Before I realized that love was there to love me back, it almost slipped between my fingers. I couldn't run fast enough to the courthouse to complete my divorce papers. I prayed to God for guidance and asked Him if this was the right thing for me to do because I was hurting inside. I was at the point of no return. I wanted my freedom. I wanted to find that happy person inside.

I wasn't comfortable staying at my sister's home, invading her space with her and her husband, so I decided to spend most of my time at my mother's studio apartment; which was in the same complex as my sister's. I slept almost every other night on my mother's couch. I talked to her about the decision I made to file for divorce. She was very supportive through the entire process. She helped calm my fears and doubts; but things were about to change and change fast. I went to work every day and some days turned into nights. So, life began to change dramatically as I continued to travel my road; I wasn't sure of the outcome, or even if I would make it. I just knew that whatever road I traveled, God was surly to be there in the midst. For you to really see the road that I traveled, you must go back in time with me to the very beginning of the whole journey.

(Brother/Age/6)/Far/right(StepFather/Deceased "Rest in Peace") James, (Me, age 5) bottom and (Mother)

CHAPTER 2

CHOOSING
MY MAN

As I entered the school bus, I noticed the bus smelled like cologne. The fragrance lingered in the air and pinpointed my nose. "God forgive me," I said to myself as my flesh began to rise. I sat right in front of the person that smelled so good. He went to school with me when we were in the ninth grade, and now we were in the eleventh grade. "I think I should get to know him a little better," I told myself.

He had on the nicest clothes, a cream dress shirt and matching pants. He looked as if he was ready for church, but of course he wasn't because we were on our way to school. I couldn't help just staring at him, checking him out from top to bottom. His hair was so neatly combed; it looked as if he just cut it out of a magazine and glued it to his head. He was the only kid in the school I saw bring the "afro" back. The bus moved on as we traveled to school on that nice sunny day. That was my first impression.

I just had to find out more about that guy because he was so nice looking. The thought crossed my mind after school when the bell rang in sixth period. I couldn't wait to jump on the bus and sit behind that young man with the skin-crawling cologne. I stared at him and watched him for a few days to see if he was different from the other boys in school who thought they were thugs.

I ran home wondering if I was ready for a boyfriend. He looked like a good person to me. I didn't consider what God was thinking, nor did I ask God if this person was the one for me. I thought I could make the decision on my own and God would agree with me.

I went to church every Sunday, Tuesday, and anytime the doors of the church were opened. I was there singing in the choir and giving God all the praise. I had a relationship with God, and my plan was not to break it. I was in love with the Lord, but little did I know, I was thinking more and more about the young boy than God.

The following weeks of school, I still hadn't gotten enough courage to talk to him. I found out his name from a girl on the bus; his name was Brandon. She told me he just broke up with this other girl on the bus named Kiki. I didn't care, but the thought was good! He was single and fine, I could finally make a move. The bell rang and I ran quickly to the bus to make sure no one else sat next to him. When I got to the seat behind him, he was alone. I waited until the bus started and then I made my move. "Hey, what's up Brandon?" I asked. "Why do you always sit alone on the bus?" He replied by saying he liked having his own seat. He then asks me why I was sitting alone and I told him, "No reason." I decided since he seemed like a nice person, I had to ask him what he was doing later to make small conversation.

"Nothing," he replied.

There was a pause for a minute and I thought, "Man, this is harder than I thought, this boy is so shy and if he keeps giving me short answers, I am not going to have very much to say." I wasn't going to give up that easily. Our stop was just seconds away and I had to think of something quick.

"Hey, I challenge you to a game of basketball." I said. "I know you like to play, and I played a little on the team, so what do you say?"

"Okay" was his one-word response.

I hurried and jotted down my number on a sheet of paper and gave it to him and told him he had to call me to set up a time to meet at the park.

I waited anxiously by the phone because my mother taught me not to call the guy, but to let him call. It seemed as if time went so slowly and wasn't moving at all. Finally, the phone rang and I ran to it. I answered as if I wasn't sitting around waiting for him to call. I could hear the fear in his voice as if I was going to come through the phone and bite him. I couldn't believe how shy he was; I had to hold in my laughter while he gave me the time to go to the park. That was the day I would never forget. I was hooked after that day. We talked on the phone every night after school, and I just knew I was in love; or so I thought.

He came to my home to meet my mother and I went to his home to meet his family. The first thing my mother told me after she met him was, "Don't let that holding of hands get you in a lot of trouble."

I remember saying "Mom, you don't have anything to worry about; holding hands doesn't mean I am going to want to have sex." "Well, in my book it does," she replied. My mother was very old school when it came down to dating and having a boyfriend. I was seventeen-years old and still a virgin. I thought I would be fine because God was on my side and He was my strength. Surely, He would help me keep my virginity.

I asked Brandon a lot of things about school, college, and what plans he had for his life. He told me he wanted to pursue a career in animals, and then maybe in the future he would be able to open his own business. I was excited because our dreams were similar. I wanted to go to a community college and then maybe a university and then start my career. I wanted to own my own home one day, get married and have about three to four children and have a business to support my family. I had it all planned and I finally had someone on my side who said they wanted similar things. My emotions felt even stronger for Brandon after he told me that.

We were the "couple of our class" the year 2000, and all the girls were envious of me and the guys were jealous of him. We spent all the time we could together in and out of school. My mother started telling us we were spending too much time together but I couldn't get enough of Brandon. We had been going out now for seven months; we declared our love for each other and talked about getting married one day. I thought about him so much, I decided to keep a journal to release my thoughts so I wouldn't drive myself crazy thinking too much. Keeping a journal was the best thing I could have done, because Brandon began asking me for sex and sex was the last thing on my mind.

Friday, July 7, 1999
2:00p.m.

Dear Diary,

Here I am, at home not knowing what to think, pretending to speak directly to Brandon to help ease the tension. I've told you how I feel about having sex before marriage, but it seems like the importance of this matter is not your concern. I can't say any more than what I know to say and that is what I believe in. I have kept my promises to you and I have made up my mind. I am going to keep my promise to God. It makes me a better person to know right and to apply it to my life. You have told me you love me, and many might ask me how I know, and it's because you have shown me with your actions. Everything you do reflects what you tell me. That is the same thing as me telling you that I love you, and showing you. I have told you that God is first in my life. I have shown you that as well, and if you don't see these things, then I must check myself and start walking the talk and not just talking the talk. I love you Brandon, but everything that feels good is not good for you. I hate that we must have a disagreement about sex, but we must deal with it if we choose to do it in the first place.

I would rather not have sex than to have it and be emotionally broken inside and spiritually impaired. What I mean is, I could go ahead and do it and still be physically hurt just to make you feel good, or I could avoid all the hurt and pain and not have sex. "Sex is one true fire," my mother told me, "that can never be put out, you can never satisfy that person and the fire keeps burning and burning." So, what should we do about this? We should make the decision for less pain and less hardship regarding our relationship and our minds. If we want to take on sex, we must deal with everything that comes with it, because it wasn't made for kids! We can't get married right now, so we should decide if we want the consequences and the reality.

The thought of telling him all I was thinking kept coming but nothing really resulted from all my pleading and begging in my diary. I continued to write. *Baby, we have been together for seven months and yes, it's been hard these last couple of months but we don't have to make it harder for ourselves. We can make this relationship as hard as we want or as smooth as possible. It's just the things we must accept or the things we must do to make our relationship what we want it to be. Today we talked about what privileges you have as being my boyfriend. You know you can ask my parents to take me anywhere as long as it is decent, we can go. I don't want this relationship to fall apart because we have our own perspective on things. Sometimes, our own perspective can get in the way of our understanding each other.*

These were the thoughts that I most desperately wanted to get off my shoulders and tell him, but it was easier for me to put them on paper. I thought our love was unpredictable, but real. I wanted our relationship to last and be successful; but we continued to have our differences, and we seemed to disagree more and more every day. I can't remember the times when we didn't argue or disagree on something. That was a sign that our days together were going to get more and more stressful. I knew from the very beginning that he didn't want anything more in life than what he already had. He felt he was happy with the way his life was and there wasn't a need for him to try and reach for anything more. He told me one thing in the beginning just to keep me, but meant something else once he had me.

That was not the ideal relationship I had in mind. I felt that love would keep us together, and maybe in the future it would all change. Time seemed to pass by so fast and my love grew more and more for him. Our differences began to grow as well. I felt like I was battling between good and evil. I was fighting my flesh every day not to give in to the calling of sex and his desires of wanting me. He was asking me almost every day to have sex with him and I didn't know if I could hold out any longer. The aggravation and pressure from Brandon was pulling at my spirit and my mind. I was almost screaming inside not knowing what I should do.

My mother taught me that God wanted us to keep our virginity until marriage and that was what I truly wanted to do. I wanted to be blessed when I got married. I wanted to walk down the aisle in my white dress letting the world see me, well, not really the world. God had a calling on my life and I knew it. However, I was in a constant battle with myself and I was distracted from hearing God's voice. I thought I could handle a relationship with a boy and serve the true and most high God.

What I failed to realize was that the person I chose to be with, wanted me to choose him over God, and I did.

I made a big mistake that would take me on a journey of my breaking point. I never thought I would choose to be in love and fight to continue to have the divine love of God. I had my signals crossed and it could have killed me.

My relationship became more and more controlling and I didn't even see it. All I saw was love. I was so wrapped up in love, that the exact signs I warned myself of in my diary blinded me. I told myself that a relationship couldn't be based on feelings and lust. I also said God must be first in my life and both he and I must agree when choosing a mate. I told myself these things, but ignored them all just to please Brandon, who by the way was not thinking about pleasing God, or me. He wanted to please his flesh. He had sex on the brain twenty-four/seven, and I didn't know what to do next, but give in.

One day in school, he had been writing me little love letters about how he wanted to make love to me and how much he loved me. He went on and on about it. I just got so tired of hearing it; I decided to give in to his calls. While we were walking home that same day I thought, "How bad could it be? He says he loves me, I know he would take his time and not hurt me." We went into my house and my mother wasn't home yet. I made myself act as if directing the whole thing didn't scare me, but deep down inside I knew I was going straight to hell.

I lay down on the bed and watched as he tried to put a condom on. It was so funny, I couldn't help but laugh, but things soon became no laughing matter.

A few minutes passed, but it felt like hours. As he poked to find the spot to put his penis, I squirmed and whined in pain. I whispered in his ear, "Let's stop because it is not going to go in." He immediately grabbed the sheets to get a good grip and pushed in with such a force, I screamed. I screamed so loud it scared him and probably the neighbors too. I threw him off me and we both fell to the floor. I remembered the excruciating pain that followed, with blood everywhere. There was blood all over the sheets, bed, and the floor. The pain just wouldn't stop. He tried to comfort me but it didn't work. I immediately pushed him out of the house to leave me alone. I didn't want him to touch me or talk to me. I couldn't believe that was my first time, the time that was supposed to be a wonderful experience, a time I'd remember for the rest of my life." I thought to myself, "what a waste." I finally gave in to condemning myself to hell and now I had a horrible day to remember for the rest of my life. I couldn't sleep or face myself in the mirror. It only took forty-eight hours for me to call Brandon and tell him I was okay.

I thought that maybe since our little plan of making love didn't turn out the way we planned, then maybe he would finally listen to me and not want to have sex until marriage. I was still hoping to redeem myself from what I knew would condemn me. I didn't want to have sex in the first place, but I was suddenly starting to feel that I needed to please him. I didn't want him to be mad at me. "How would we be the happy couple if I couldn't make him happy?" I kept thinking of ways to try to make him happy without the sex, but he just didn't let up. Not even two weeks went by and he was begging again. There was no doubt in my mind that he wasn't going to give up. I gave in again. He had no trouble finding my spot nor did he want to use a condom. He had more trouble putting the condom on than making his way in. I felt I was trapped, but I convinced myself again that I was in love.

I just knew that I was pregnant every time we did it, even though it was all in my head. I didn't know the facts of how sperm worked but I did know if it got in me, I could be pregnant. I didn't want that, especially since I was so close to being eighteen and graduating from high school. Our relationship began to change even more because he was getting the release of testosterone. I didn't recognize him anymore. He changed for the worst. It just kept getting worse it seemed, for I just couldn't understand what Brandon wanted me to do any more.

The more I did for him, the less I did for myself and the less he did for me. I went to church less and I didn't understand why. I couldn't feel my own heart beat anymore. I wanted to disappear from this world of unhappiness. I was giving him my all, but all he wanted to give me in return was sex. I stopped wanting to feel that great feeling of making love. That was not what we were doing anyway. I knew there was a difference between, sex and lovemaking. I even tried to explain it to him by telling him he needed to be more compassionate about my feelings and my emotions. All he would say was I was the one with the problems and if I didn't give him sex, I wasn't doing my girlfriend duties. My girlfriend duties! He acted as if I was his sex project, and that was what I was supposed to do at all time; even during my period.

Emotionally, I began to fade. I started convincing myself that I loved him even more. I was blinded by the thought of love and the idea of being loved. I had my signals twisted again because I wasn't getting what I called "love" in return. We continued to argue every day and it just wouldn't let up. I prayed for understanding on why we couldn't get along. I began to write in my diary even more in hope of finding a solution to the problem, but all it did was lead to more misunderstanding and a breakup.

December 6, 1999
9:05p.m.

Dear Diary,

Here I am sitting in my room pondering how Brandon and I got together and how you really know when you love someone. I remember when I thought I was in love, and come to find out, I was deeply in like. How can I tell the difference? Well, first, it's taking me forever to try not to think of him or feel the love I have for him. Looking at his picture at night brings tears to my eyes wishing that things were like they used to be; walking through the halls every day together, holding hands and giving each other a kiss before I entered my class. Now I am the one watching the other couples as they stroll down the hallway in my direction, it seems the couples are laughing in my face. The more I think of him, the more I get knots in my stomach. Eleven months we walked the halls holding hands, hugging and kissing each other, never leaving each other's side without telling the other how much we loved each other. Now that we have separated, I feel my world is upside down.

I felt my world was so sad without the love of my life, but little did I know the breakup would only last a month. He came back to me and told me that he wanted to be with me and start over. I forgave him for his behavior of wanting sex so much and hoped that he would see it my way; but little did I know he would want it even more. We began where we left off. The arguments didn't stop; but started all over again. He disagreed about me going to church all the time, and he hated me telling him I didn't want to have sex.

I felt like I was back with the person I wanted to be with, but not where I wanted to be. I wanted to feel that love and happiness, that was so sweet, like in our first seven months of dating. I had hoped that God would change him and we would be happy. I decided to start thinking more about the future and how I wanted to live my life. I wanted to be happy and go to college, then get married and have children. He said he wanted the same things in the beginning of our relationship, but he eliminated the three most crucial factors I wanted. He told me that he no longer wanted to go to college. He didn't know when he wanted to get married and he only wanted one child or none. I couldn't believe what I was hearing after all the time that had passed; he never told me the truth.

He led me to believe he wanted the same things I wanted. The love I felt didn't feel like love anymore. It started to feel like obligation and betrayal. I felt I was deceived into loving him and the person that I cared so much for was not that person at all. He was a totally different person, a stranger. Yet, I felt there might have been a change or a chance that he would change his mind and become the person he told me he was. A month had gone by and nothing had changed in my favor. Sex was still asked for and I still gave. He was not letting up and I was almost at the point of not arguing about it anymore.

I decided to take over my thoughts and plan for the marriage I wanted since we had been dating a year and a half. I wrote on a pad: *before and after marriage concerns and questions.* It was a way to analyze what we had in common and what we didn't have in common. It was also a road map for me to see if we were marriage material. I continued to write: *getting married can't be because you are pregnant, by yourself, or want to get out of your parent's house. You can't have a marriage when one person wants to go one way and the other wants to go another way. Real love is trust, respect, and caring. Friendship is trust and when you are going through problems in your relationship, you must have effective communication. It would be wise to postpone both marriage and living together if one wants to get married and the other thinks simply living together would be better.* Living together is one of the most common things to do when people are in a relationship and I didn't believe in it.

I wanted to make sure I could be honest with myself by writing down concerns and questions and answering them. By doing that, it gave me the answers I needed to avoid making possible mistakes or so I thought. So, I continued with the list: What are the concerns and questions of my qualifying mate?

Concerns	*Questions*
If you share the same interest.	*Do you argue, fight, or disagree on almost everything?*
If you cannot talk and be open.	*What will the both of you do when one is spending more than you must spend?*

If you feel comfortable around certain people and your mate does not.	*How will both want to raise the children? Will it be the same?*
Personality, responsibility, and intimacy play a key role.	*Will there be discipline or not?*
If both of you have different views on working and spending time at home, that could become a potential problem.	*Do the both of you plan or is one living for the moment?*
If there is a different view on having things split down the middle, fifty-fifty or is it unified....	*Who will do the housework, cooking, cleaning, and taking care of the bills?*

When deciding on the person to marry, find out as much as you can before marriage. The dislikes and likes of your mate will and can break a marriage if there is not a compromise or understanding in the beginning.

I could go on and on about the things I wrote down for myself to answer. Unfortunately, I didn't even follow my own directions. I didn't listen to my own advice I placed in front of me. I wanted to have a successful marriage and I wanted it to include the positive things not the negative things. After writing all my thoughts on paper, I never went back to look at them again. I didn't even look at them when I needed them the most. That's when everything failed. I thought I had everything I needed to know in my mind and I felt it would come into play when I needed it.

It didn't work. I pressed forward with my eyes closed believing that what I had I could change. "I could make him a better person. I have Christ in my life and if I keep witnessing to him, he would come around and we will live happily-ever after." I told myself. I began to think I could give him a little information from time to time and soon he would see it the way I saw it. Yet he never seemed to get it. As much as I tried to give him the positive information about being a couple, the more we disagreed. The more I told him about Christ the more he didn't want to hear it. I couldn't believe it. Yet, I wasn't going to give up on him, because he was my high school sweetheart. I felt I was supposed to marry him; I was in love with him.

I wouldn't let up on myself about the way I felt about him. The more we argued, the more I forgave him. I couldn't find it in my heart to tell him that he wasn't the one for me. I knew deep down inside, but I didn't want to face it. I didn't want to be alone and feel that void and loneliness that I felt when we broke up before. So, I kept all those doubts in and told myself it was just a matter of time before we came around; little did I know, I would become pregnant before we came around.

Two months passed by since we got back together and there were only two months left until graduation. I started to feel sick and nauseous and just I knew I was pregnant. I thought I was pregnant every time we had sex, but that time was different. My period was late and it had not come on in one week. My period was never late. I was scared to death. There I was: eighteen years old, still living at home, about to graduate, and there was a great possibility I was pregnant. "I don't want this to be. I want to go to college, to be married first, oh please Lord don't let this be happening to me." I couldn't wait two weeks to take a test. I had a bad feeling that I was pregnant and I knew Brandon was not going to be happy.

The emotions and feelings of fear ran through my veins. I wanted to scream and disappear all at the same time. I wanted to do just that when I called Brandon on the phone. I tried to convince myself he would tell me everything would be okay and we would get through it together. I wanted it all to go away. I had no one to turn to but God and my diary. I needed to get my feelings off my chest and I needed to call Brandon and tell him what was up.

March 01, 2000
7:55p.m.

Dear Diary,

Here I am in my room, thinking about fifteen minutes ago when I got off the phone with Brandon. I tried to hint to him that I was feeling sick and he acted as if he didn't know what I was talking about. So, I told him that my period still hasn't come on and it has been one month. He became so angry. He yelled at me on the phone saying he didn't want to hear it or think about it. Then he said, "You just want to be pregnant, because you are always telling me this." Here I am, trying to get support because I am scared to death. I'm not sure how many days I am late anymore; all I know is, last month I went off on the 28th or so, because this month I haven't had a drop. I know I should have come on by now and went off, because February was the short month. I don't know what to think! I do know, I can't talk to him and I don't want to talk to anyone else until I know for sure. I just know if I am, talking to somebody else will just make the situation worse. I didn't want to have sex on Valentine's Day, but he insisted, and I am supposed to be the one who wants to be pregnant? Who's the one trying not to have sex, and who's the one who just must have it? If he wants to blame somebody, he needs to blame himself. I can't take this! I must call him back.

I called him back that night and we argued all night about the way I felt and how he didn't want any kids because he was still a child himself. He went on and on about how it was my fault I was feeling the way I felt and until I had any proof I was pregnant, he didn't want to talk about it. I said, "Fine, I'll go to the store and get a test." I couldn't help but ask him if he would be with me while I took it. He said, "No," so I went alone.

I remember how I felt walking into the store. It was as though everyone in the whole store was watching me. I walked slowly around the counters and the long way up and down the wrong aisles until I got enough courage to go to the aisles where they kept the pregnancy tests. I was scared out of my mind. My heart was beating out of my chest and it seemed like everyone was yelling "Shame on you," It was all in my head. As I reached the checkout counter, I couldn't bear the thought that my future was going to change dramatically.

I held the test in my hand hoping and praying that it would say "negative" without me even taking it out of the box. Finally, I made my way to the restroom that was located at the entrance of the store. I entered inside and it felt as if I had walked into a freezer, for my heart froze. I looked under all the stalls and no one was there. I locked the door behind me so no one could enter.

I went into the biggest stall and took the test. As I waited, I just stared at the wall hoping that nothing would show positive. I think thirty seconds went by, and then one minute and I couldn't wait any longer, so I looked. Oh, my God! I was pregnant. I thought I was so dead. I couldn't move. I held the test in my hand crying and wiping the tears from my face. I didn't want to be pregnant. I was a Christian girl and I wanted to go to college, but now I had a baby inside of me. Finally, after talking to myself I got enough courage to go home.

I called Brandon and gave him the news. He didn't believe me. I told him that I had the test in my hand and that he could come over and see it himself. He did. However, he still wanted more proof. I said to him, "How much more proof do you need?" He exclaimed he wanted a doctors' word. I told him I knew the perfect place we could get a test done free.

He agreed to take me to the women's center. They tested women of all ages who thought they were pregnant. The nurse came in the room and asked both of us to fill out long applications so she could better understand the situation. It felt like hours passed. We waited for the nurse to test me. We sat in a little waiting room decorated with baby toys and baby clothes. The items were available if needed. Brandon rocked his legs up and down in nervousness. I knew he was hoping for a negative answer. Finally, the nurse called me into the room to take the test. We knew from that point that we had at least five minutes to wait for the results. Time seemed to pass slowly. We sat there anticipating the results.

The nurse walked in and told us to follow her to another room to receive the results of the pregnancy test. Waiting in the room was a nicely dressed lady with the results of the test in her hands. We had an idea of what she was about to say, but we had no idea it would be so extreme. "Yes, you both are pregnant, and you are six weeks along," she said. I couldn't believe my ears when she said, "six weeks along." That was a month and a half. No wonder I felt the way I did. Brandon was not happy at all. He walked out while the lady was talking. I couldn't believe he was so rude, thinking only of himself.

He sat in the car swearing and yelling at himself. He turned to me as I got in the car and said, "Let's get an abortion." "Abortion, are you crazy?" You know I don't believe in abortions. Why would you want to kill this innocent baby, your baby?" I yelled.

"It's not a baby yet, it's just a sack," he replied.

"You are crazy. No, I am not killing our child!" We went home very scared that day not knowing what our parents were going to say about the whole situation.

We were only two months from graduation and we would be officially considered adults. However, we were already adults and parents to be.

When we got to our homes we told our parents separately that we were pregnant. He said his mother took it well and I told him the same. We were on our own and we had to come up with all the money ourselves to cover the expenses we accumulated. I decided to do the math just to see how much money we needed before the baby arrived. I slowly thought it out and came up with twenty-six hundred dollars just to have the baby. That came to three hundred plus dollars a month for seven months.

Time went on and I got bigger and bigger. Brandon and I continued to have our differences, and expressed them by arguing. I didn't understand why we didn't get along when the signs were clear. We had nothing in common and we desired two different futures. I wanted to accomplish my goals in life and make them come true through challenging work and perseverance.

He wanted to work every day, nine-to-five and leave everything just as it was for as long as it could. If change didn't come and take over, then he was not going to change anything. He wanted me to give up my dreams of making a lot of money and owning property to pass down to our children. I wasn't going to do that.

I still wanted to have him around me to support me with our child. I longed to have a husband that I could raise my child with and I wanted it to be Brandon. I still loved him and I felt that one day he would change. We made it through graduation, with no one noticing, May of 2000! It was a relief for the both of us.

He wanted to please me, so he tried to make every doctor's appointment. I thought he was beginning to see how much I needed him. However, we still did not get along through the whole nine months, but I was happy because he tried. I thought he changed and was growing up and ready to be the father that our child needed. We had our beautiful son October 2000.

He came in weighing seven pounds, thirteen ounces, and twenty-one inches long. That was the most wonderful and painful experience I had ever felt. There was joy finally holding the baby that lived inside of me so long. I had my son in my arms and I now was a mother. I no longer felt the fear of motherhood and was ready to take care of my son with all my might. I only needed one thing and that was Brandon to stay by my side and be there for us no matter what.

CHAPTER 3

SPIRITUAL LOSS AND AN EMOTIONAL ROLLERCOASTER

I couldn't seem to separate my spirituality from the sin of having sex unmarried. Every time we had sex I could feel my spirit dampen and my soul became more buried inside myself. I could feel the connection I had with God fade away and the connection with my inner self become an emotional rollercoaster.

I didn't want to disappoint God. However, I chose to please man when I let Brandon enter my body and defile my soul. My soul was hungry all the time to be refilled by the Holy Spirit but I kept feeding my flesh sin. I searched for the love of my man to fill the love that I had for God and it made the hole I had in my heart bigger.

I let the emotions of "love" take over my mind, body, and soul. I no longer had faith that God was on the throne. I started to trust in myself. I failed at everything I tried to do; whether it was on my job, at home or in my struggle walking with God. Nothing seemed to line up because I placed a person in such high esteem. I gave away something more precious than sex. I gave away the communion I had with my Spiritual Father.

My world was now turned upside down and now I felt cursed. I couldn't see the curse and all that it had in store for me, but what I did see was the continuation of pain, unhappiness and sex. It became apparent that the love I thought I had for Brandon was consuming me and I didn't know how to rescue myself from the sin I was in.

It got so bad that I began to despise the very thing that got me into the sin in the first place, myself. I also began to despise Brandon. I hated the idea or thought of having sex.

It literally made me emotionally, physically, and spiritually sick. Every time we had sex, it became more and more painful.

He would enter my body and the pain would be unbearable. It would hurt so bad that I would cry and plead with him to stop.

He never understood the physical pain that he was putting me through, so he wouldn't stop. He said that he wasn't hurting me and it was all in my head. I began to not like him very much, yet I wanted to please him. I wondered how he could love me and cause me so much pain. How could he continue to get pleasure out of something that hurt me?

I began to believe he was very selfish and all he thought about was him-self. Brandon didn't love me nor did he care about me. I didn't understand why he wanted to hurt me. I thought maybe it was just me. I was confused, but I believed I was beginning to understand. He wanted to take over my body and use it for his pleasure. The more I backed off, the more he wanted me. I realized that the four years we had been together were based on his needs. When he decided what he wanted and how he wanted it, I no longer mattered. I had also pushed myself to the side and did not even realize it.

I worked harder and harder every day to explain to him that the physical pain I felt was real. He kept telling me it was my imagination and that I needed to get my head checked. I knew what he was saying. I got myself checked and it wasn't in my head.

I asked my doctor why did I continue to have pain during sex and he didn't give me the answer I wanted to hear. The Doctor told me I had a bacterial infection or a bad yeast infection. He gave me some creams and called it a day.

I was very disturbed after the visit. I just knew something else was wrong and that maybe the doctor looked over it. The creams did their jobs, but the pain never seemed to go away. I had so much medicine in my cabinets that I felt as if I was a cream puff. I didn't know what to think or do next. I couldn't call or tell anyone because no one understood my body.

I was alone in my own world of pain and misery. My mother wasn't there to comfort me nor was my brothers or sister. They were consumed in their own lives. There I was, struggling to figure out what was wrong with my body and I had no one to turn to. I felt that God stopped hearing my prayers, and I almost stopped praying. I asked God to have mercy on my soul and to forgive me for the sins I had committed and to spare me. I wanted to be happy and free.

Even though we had our first child, our relationship didn't change. Sex didn't change either. Brandon on the other hand, did change. After the baby was born, he wanted a new companion, a dog. He always told me he couldn't get a dog as a child, and now that he was nineteen and grown, he wanted one.

I never agreed on a dog, but I told him to wait until the baby was a little older. Our baby was only two weeks old and I knew I would be the one watching over the dog if we got one.

Without even consulting me he went out and bought a two-hundred-dollar dog. He put the dog in a cage inside the room with the baby and me. I was furious. We had a child and he wanted to be a child. He wanted to turn back the hands of time and pretend he had no responsibilities and no baby to care for. We argued about the dog but he kept it. Not even three months went by and he went out and got two more dogs to fulfill his desires. I hadn't moved out of my mother's home and now it was my mother, her husband, the baby, and me, with the dogs in the home.

I couldn't believe it, and I wasn't powerful enough to control the situation. The only thing I could think of doing was to yell and fuss and tell him that in three months I was moving out of my parents' home and the dogs had to go. He agreed to get rid of all the dogs, but he was not very happy with me about the situation.

I told him there would be other times when he could get his dogs and raise them, but this was not the time. I continued to pressure him about trying to spend more time with his son and me instead of his friends from school. He didn't see it though, because the more I told him, the less he would come to my mother's home to visit. I didn't know what to think anymore. I did know that it was time for him to grow up and be a man.

My first apartment came through and I was happy. I was on my own and doing for myself. I didn't have to worry about depending on my mother's home or taking care of Brandon's dogs.

He came and got rid of the dogs and I was ready to take on the world with a bang! I still wanted us to be the ideal family since we had a child together, but I didn't want to shack up (live together without being married). I felt that if we were to shack up, then he would never commit to marriage.

He told me that it would be better if we just lived together than to get married. Reason being, we could test it out first and if we didn't like it, then we could part. I knew deep down inside he was afraid of commitment. I needed to show him that commitment was simple and that he just needed to do it. I waited and waited for him to ask me to marry him and he never did, so when he asked to move in with me six months later, I gave in to him instead.

I thought for a moment that it would be great, the both of us raising our son together doing what parents do as a couple. It wasn't that at all. Brandon wanted to live the life of a young teenager while I was the working housemother. He would stay out late at night and when he didn't work, he would eat up the food and not want to replace it.

He would come home and mess up the house with his dirty clothes and shoes and not pick up after himself. I couldn't believe what I saw. I didn't know he was the way he was, nor did I know I would be the one to clean up after him. I thought he was totally different because he came from his mother's clean home. I was not ready to be a maid, but I didn't want him to break up with me. I tried to make it work. We still seemed to have different views on everything and it appears we wouldn't be together long. A couple of months went by and there was a disturbance in the apartment building next to us.

We both didn't want to live there anymore, so I decided to move back into my parents' home while they moved into another home next door. I was happy. We both decided to stay at our own parent's home for three weeks until everything was settled.

When the three weeks went by, we were back on the saddle and ready to continue to live in the world of sin. I still couldn't get it out of my head that we were shacking up and that we could perhaps burn in hell, if we didn't get it together and get married. I decided to bring marriage to the table again. This time it was an ultimatum.

I felt that he was taking advantage of my body, my house, my time and my love. It was time for him to own up to his responsibilities. I waited for one whole month before bringing up the ultimatum just to see if my mind was playing tricks on me. I wanted to make sure I felt the way I did.

During the month I was thinking, I went to the doctor because I was still having pains. The doctor told me I had a pelvic inflammatory infection, which was caused by more bacteria. I couldn't understand why I kept getting infections. When I confronted Brandon about the possibility of him cheating, he denied ever cheating. I had no proof, so I couldn't really accuse him of cheating, other than the horrible pain I felt. I just left it alone and continued our everyday life. The doctor told us there should be no sexual intercourse for three weeks because I could get pregnant in my fallopian tubes. I was thrilled that I didn't have to go through the pain, but I was furious that he gave me the infection.

During the last week of my no contact rule, Brandon was dying to have sex. I told him that if we were to have sex, I could get pregnant and that it could be harmful to me. I really didn't want to feel more pain. I wanted to be free of sex period but pleasing him was my weakness. He told me that he would stop if it hurt and that he would pull out to make sure that he didn't release inside of me. I told him that he was taking a significant risk and that if I were to get pregnant, he would have to take responsibility for his actions. He assured me that he would pull out but soon after, I heard him say, "I'm sorry it slipped." I couldn't believe it. He gave me his word and then did it anyway. We argued that day. I told Brandon that I was pregnant and he said I was crazy.

I waited a full month and went to the doctor to see just how crazy I was. I wasn't crazy at all. I was four weeks pregnant and the test didn't lie. I went to him and told him that I was pregnant and the room got very quiet.

It was as though he was about to cry. Then suddenly, he grabbed my leg and begged me to abort the baby. I told him that he was out of his mind. How could he ask me to abort our second child when he didn't want the first? I couldn't believe he would even ask me to do that again. I was hurt and furious. I didn't know what to think. All I could remember was letting him have it about being a man. I wanted to have a real family. I wanted to take on Brandon's last name and call him my husband. I was tired. I didn't want to any longer have all his babies and be his maid. I knew that I was worth more than just having babies. I wanted more. I wanted it right then and there.

I told him that he had a choice to either marry me or he could move out and go back home with his mother. I didn't want to keep having children out of wedlock. I wanted a husband to help me raise the kids and support me through the hard times. I wanted an answer right then and there.

He hesitated, and the more he waited the more demanding I got. I didn't want to lie up next to a man who was not my husband. I was tired, and for some reason, I thought that marriage was the answer. My mother told me that if I didn't get married, that I needed to get out of sin. The pressure was on. I didn't know what else to do, but to keep at him.

I walked outside for a minute to take a break from all the arguing. I went back inside the house to let him know what I was thinking. I told Brandon that I could call the pastor to arrange a meeting to set up marriage counseling if he wanted to get married.

If not, he could pack his things now and go back to his mother's. He agreed to go to counseling but I knew inside he was scared to death and a little hesitant. I didn't understand why he was so afraid to commit, when we were already living life as a married couple.

I knew that Brandon still wanted to have his friends and do what he wanted without feeling obligated to me as a husband but that didn't change what I wanted. He told me many times that if he was to get married, he would feel locked down and he didn't want that. He listened to all his single friends that told him that if he were to get married, he would be locked down forever. I disagreed. I assured him that marriage was a companionship and not jail. We still were not on the same page, but he agreed. He wanted to be with me and agreed that we should get our marriage license to seal the deal.

I was excited. We were finally going to tie the knot after four years. It was going to be official. I remember when we received the license. The lady at the office told us we had ninety days to get married or the license would be void and we'd lose the money we paid. It didn't seem as though he cared too much about losing the money because after two months went by, we still had not married. I went to him and told him that we were running out of time and if we didn't get married within the month, then we would lose the license. Again, he hesitated. I couldn't help but remember I was pregnant *again* and I didn't want to be bare foot and pregnant living in sin. I couldn't keep living the way we were. I told Brandon that he needed to decide. I was furious. Brandon finally agreed to finalize the marriage. I said, "Great, we will do it this Sunday, March 2002." He about swallowed his tongue, "Why so soon?" He asked.

We started arguing again about the same thing. I could clearly see that he did not want to marry me, but I just wouldn't let up. I wanted so badly to get right with God; I wasn't hearing the man I wanted to marry telling me directly to let him go.

He wanted out, but he didn't want to be alone. He wanted to have me, but he didn't want to marry me. It was so confusing. I didn't know what to do other than stick to my gut and keep giving him an ultimatum about marriage or the highway.

When Sunday arrived for us to get married, he was dragging around the house. He said that he was sick and didn't want to go to church. I asked him, "If we don't go to the church, then how are we going to get married?"

He said he didn't care. He went on to say, "I want to get married in the office with just you, me and the Pastor. I don't want everyone to see us get married." I thought he was crazy! I questioned him out of shock.

"We are getting married, yet you are telling me you don't want anyone to see us get married?" "I do and I want to walk down the aisle. This is supposed to be the happiest day of our lives and you are messing it up!" I was in tears. I didn't know what to do. Then when I thought all couldn't get worse, it kept getting worse. It was passed time to leave and church was almost over and I couldn't find the keys to the car. Brandon wanted to drive his car and I wanted to drive my car. At that point, we did not like each other, yet we still were getting married. After thirty minutes of looking for the car keys, I finally found them and we rushed to the church.

I felt we were making a great big mistake. However, I still wanted to complete the marriage process, hoping that everything would work and finally redeem me of all my sinful ways. After that day, we were finally husband and wife.

Everything changed dramatically. Brandon let me know he still didn't want to be married and he clearly expressed it. The night of our marriage, he didn't even want to make love and I finally wanted to, go figure. Finally, this was the night we were supposed to come together as one and finally make love and he leaves the house. He spent half of the night with his friends and made sure he stayed away from me as much as possible.

Not even two weeks passed and he decides to buy a dog to replace the dogs he had before. He decides to blame me for getting rid of the first dogs, so the replacement was supposed to justify his actions. I told him to keep the dog if it was going to make him happy. I told him I wouldn't mind having a little dog of my own.

That way the kids could play with it since he chose such a dangerous breed for himself. I saw the cutest little dog and thought it would be perfect for the kids. I wanted to do whatever I thought would keep us from arguing but it just seemed no matter what I tried, we still couldn't see eye to eye. Once I got my dog, I realized we were going to have a conflict. He didn't want me telling him anything about raising his dog. He wanted to raise it on his own. I just didn't get it! The job he was doing was sad!

He would let the dog stay in his pin all day with poop all over it. I questioned him, "Why wouldn't you train the dog and then put him in a cage?" he would respond in a smart way. He told me that just because I paper-trained my dog; it didn't mean that he didn't know what he was doing. I just shook my head in disgust and left him alone.

Brandon's dog became very wild and disobedient because he didn't teach it anything. I just laughed inside thinking that he was going to have a tough time raising that dog. He just wanted to do everything the way he wanted and my suggestions meant nothing.

He still wouldn't come home before the sun went down and I wouldn't stop nagging him about not spending time with us. He just didn't want anything to do with his family. I knew it, but he denied it. I remained in the house all-day on one of my days off. When he came home early-unannounced one day, I was happy and shocked to see him. He was being unusually nice that day and I just didn't understand why.

"Baby could you show me how to get to this place?" He said.

"And what place is this?" I asked.

"It is a house where some man breeds puppies." He responded.

"We don't need another dog Brandon. We have enough dogs and bills to worry about without adding another dog to the family." I said.

"I am just going to look, because my friend told me about this guy," he said.

"Okay, I will show you then." I said with suspicion.

On the way to the house I was biting my lip in expectation that he had something up his sleeve. I was not up for it at all. I just wanted peace. When we got there, I decided to stay in the car because he said he just wanted to look at the puppies. I waited and waited and then he came out of the back fence with a little fat dog. I looked at him and asked, "What are you doing with the dog?" "Isn't it cute?" He said.

"Yes, but what are you doing?" I questioned again.

"Well, I just bought him." He said. I couldn't believe what he was saying. I was about to yell at the top of my voice, but the owner was standing there. So, I just waited until we got down the road and I let it out. "How could you go and buy another dog when I told you we couldn't afford it and we didn't need another dog?" He responded by saying, "This is my money and I can do exactly what I want to do with it!" I couldn't believe what I was hearing. We had a ton of bills that weren't paid yet! "Okay, so how much did this dog cost?" He said, "It didn't cost much, just two hundred and fifty dollars." JUST TWO HUNDRED AND FIFTY DOLLARS" I yelled! "That is a lot of money that you told me you didn't have!"

I went on and on all the way home about the money that he spent on the dog. I couldn't believe it. He didn't care and there was nothing I could do.

After that day, I knew what I did or said to him didn't matter. He was going to do and say whatever he wanted no matter what. It was the beginning of war. I wasn't going to help him in any way with anything. He was a liar. He would never tell me the truth when I asked him anything. He made excuses about the money he had or didn't have and I was left paying the bills. He would go to the store for his dogs and bring back unnecessary things and I would be the one to pick up the slack. I would come home from work to his shoes, clothes, and dog poop all over the floor.

I was so stressed that I thought I was going to lose my mind. I told myself to ignore him no matter what he said to me. He wanted everything to be his way, so I let him have his way, if he didn't step on more of my toes.

One night I was relaxing at home with my dog and our fifteen-month-old son. My dog was out of her cage stretching her legs because she had been in her cage for a while. I wanted her to walk around the house. In walked Brandon and he immediately started yelling at me to put my dog in her cage because he didn't want his new dog to befriend my dog. I didn't respond to him. I just sat on the couch and ate my grapes pretending he wasn't there. He kept yelling, "you don't hear me? I know you do, put the D*** dog up or I will!" I told him, "Don't mess with my dog. She is not messing with your dog, so leave her alone."

He walked over to me and knocked the grape bowl out of my hand. I was five months pregnant at the time and was thrown off guard. I quickly jumped up and said, "Have you lost your mind? You bumped my stomach!" He still wouldn't leave the dog issue alone.

I told him that he needed to leave because he just couldn't come home demanding me to do something in my own home when he allowed his dog to poop all over the house, on clean washed clothes and wouldn't clean it up. I tried to push him out the door, but he just made his way back in. He said that he wasn't going to leave. I said, "Fine then, if you want my dog up so bad then your new dog can sleep outside." I took his dog and went to put it outside and he came up fast behind me and grabbed the back of my neck so that I would release the dog. I screamed in fear. I thought he had lost his mind for grabbing me like that.

The first thing that came to mind was to scream for my mother who lived right next door. My mother and stepfather came over all upset and yelling until I just had to walk away. They told Brandon he needed to go to his mother's house. He started yelling, "I didn't hit her, and really I didn't hit her!" I couldn't say anything else to him that night because I was so heartbroken that he would even grab me, all because of a dog.

For the next three weeks, he never came back to say he was sorry or even check on me to make sure our fifteen-month-old and unborn child were okay. Yet he made sure he came back for his dogs. He stayed at his mother's home and told them that I said he hit me. I never said he hit me. I was not only heartbroken but angry.

My mother let me crash on her couch, since she was right next door. I was so depressed and sick; I began to have problems with the baby. The doctor told me that there was a rip in the lining of the uterus and I needed to be on bed rest for one whole month. I couldn't believe it, I had to miss work and take some days off. Brandon never came by to see how I was doing.

A month went by and my friends came to my house and cleaned the entire house to make me feel better. They placed all of Brandon's dog soiled things in garbage bags and moved them on the porch. There was dog mess everywhere. It became apparent that he didn't want to live with me anymore since he never even called. I called him and told him his things were on the porch full of poop and he might want to come and get them or they wouldn't be any good.

He finally came over to place blame on me about the situation, but I wasn't in the mood to hear whose fault it might have been. All I wanted from him was an apology, but he told me instead that he wanted a divorce. I couldn't believe what I was hearing.

We had only been married two months! We had our first fight and he wanted to end it. I told him that I didn't want a divorce and I didn't want to give him one. I told him that he should think about it and reconsider.

Brandon agreed to think about it. He took the rest of his belongings and officially moved in with his mother while he thought it over. He said that since I told everyone that he hit me he didn't trust me anymore. He said that he would rather live with his mother instead of me. I tried to tell him over and over that I never said he hit me, but he wouldn't drop it.

I said, "Fine, if that is what you want to do, then you go right ahead and live with your mom, but you only have so long before you should reconsider moving back home."

He didn't understand what I meant. I explained to him that we were a married couple and that we shouldn't depend on our mothers but face this like adult and live as a married couple.

I just wanted my husband back. It appears he was gone for good and he hated me. He played the role as if he didn't want anything to do with me and continue blaming me. I started to feel exactly what he wanted me to feel, "pitiful." I was seven months pregnant and alone. I had no one to share my emotions with nor did I have the man that I desired to have. He had finally left me and I began to think I deserved it. I went through a million feelings trying to figure out what went wrong.

What was I supposed to do since my first love and only love left me, I thought? I was miserable, until one day when I looked in the mirror and realized that I was alone, but strong. I knew that I could make it on my own. I started fighting my loneliness with words of encouragement. I told myself that I was better than what I had become.

I was determined to overcome the pain of being alone. I told myself that I didn't need Brandon anymore. I told myself that if he continued to act like a child, then he only had so much time before the door would be closed forever.

I continued lifting my head up for the next two months until I gave birth to our son without him there. He weighed six pounds and three ounces. Brandon didn't bother to come to the hospital for the birth of our son.

I knew then that he still had not gotten over his selfish ways and that I could do better by myself. A week went by before he even decided to show up to see his son. He claimed that he was scared that I was going to turn him away and not let him see the baby. I told him that even though he did what he did, I still loved him and would forgive him and he could come home.

He went on to say that he wasn't ready yet and that maybe we could start out slow and then he would move back. I agreed because my heart melted and I wanted him to be in our lives.

While we supposedly worked it out from two separate homes, the days turned into nights and then we were back at each other's throats when the baby got sick. I called him and told him that our three-week-old son became very sick and the doctor admitted him in the hospital.

He told me that he had to work and couldn't miss any days of work. I yelled on the phone at him and told him that his child should come before his job and that they would understand if he would just tell them. He refused to tell his job that his son was in the hospital with pneumonia.

Yet I didn't care that I had to miss three days of work to be by my son's side. I couldn't bear to leave my son alone. I had to stay in a small room and care for my baby while the nurses gave him medicine to get well. Our fifteen-month-old son stayed with my mother until I returned. I called Brandon repeatedly so he would watch our son while I got some rest. He never came. I hadn't slept while at the hospital for three days and he refused to relieve me.

I was angry with him for neglecting his family. I wanted him to be in the kids' lives, but I knew that he had not changed. I knew that I would be the one to raise our kids alone.

I began to think about what brought us together in the first place. I could remember us at one point talking to one another, not having arguments. We used to write each other love letters, poems and sweet messages. We told each other how much we loved one another.

Going out to a movie was how we bonded together. I even thought about how long that had lasted. Seven months to be exact, I remembered. Considering the time frame, this was not long in my mind when we had been together for four years already.

What tore us apart and why we were still a part, was a constant question in my mind. I also thought about the issues that kept us apart when we were together. We had too many differences.

For one: he didn't like what I liked and lied about it in the beginning. He expected me to not want lofty expectations in life. Sex was always an issue. He wanted it and I didn't. We fussed and argued about it, but I gave in anyway. I was left alone right after, as he left to go play with his friends, like a kid. You would think if someone loves you, they would express that love directly. Not in my case.

I had spiritual battles inside, between right and wrong. When I told him about it, it just made things worse. So, I tried to limit it. He made sure his friends were first. He spent more and more time with them. He stopped taking me out altogether.

Our lives became routine: sex, T.V. and a movie; pizza and another movie, and more sex. Christianity: I was a Christian and he was not.

He felt that believing in the existence of God, was good enough for him. When we were living together, he turned the tables on me.

He began telling me that I couldn't ask or tell him to do anything, because he had a mother. Work, was an issue. I would work forty hours a week and he only worked whenever he wanted and thought that the bills wouldn't be affected by it.

There were even more issues. He would lie to me about everything. He would spend money we didn't have, on his car. I couldn't tell him anything regarding his money. I would fuss and argue all the time about these issues, thinking that maybe he would change. If I yelled and screamed and let him know what he was doing was wrong, I thought he would change.

I had to pay majority of the bills and the money he did give me, wasn't enough to cover one bill.

He would borrow money repeatedly from his mother, behind my back for god knows what. Then, pay her back behind my back, before paying our bills. I wanted him to help me around the house with anything.

I had to cook, clean up after the kids and he refused to help. I would wash all the clothes and he wouldn't lend a helping hand or say thank you. I would ask him to take out the trash and he refused to do that as well. I had to do everything. When I became upset about it, he would blame me, telling me it was my problem. When it came down to the more personal attention, again I was the cause of it. I did the foot rubs and the body massages and what did I get in return? Nothing, he would promise to give me the same and never gave it. He didn't make me feel wanted. I felt like a slave because in his mind this was what I was supposed to do. Then I asked myself, "Why did I even want him back?"

I couldn't even answer my own question. All I could think about was what I wanted. I hoped that he would be the one to give it to me. I wanted to feel like a lady. I wanted him to take me out to dinner. I couldn't remember him ever making me feel like his lady outside of high school.

Around his family, he treated me like a girlfriend, like a friend; he never addressed me as boo or baby in public. He never kissed me in the public eye, but when we got home he would be all over me. I felt like the man, taking all the responsibilities. I made sure everything was taken care of.

The kids, house, bills, was a cycle all too real. I couldn't remember him acknowledging me when I did those things.

That was my job (that's how I felt), to do what came naturally. Lovemaking was out of the picture and what I called, "painful" sex was all I received. I knew he didn't care and I was reminded every time we did it.

All those things had torn us apart. Only the opposite could bring us back together. I was tired of being so independent. I would love to be able to depend on my man, my husband. I wanted to know that he would be able to take care of the kids and me. If I lose my job, I wanted to know that he was willing to handle everything by himself; such as I had for so long. I wanted to know that he felt it was his job to do so and his responsibility to take care of the family.

This is what I wanted and hoped would happen for our family, but only time would tell and at this moment, I just didn't know what would happen.

Life is a lesson that we all must learn. We go through things to strengthen us for the next stage in our lives. We may not see the lesson while it is being taught to us.

So, once we come out, we will see that God just wanted to make us warriors for His kingdom.

CHAPTER 4

GOD IS REAL

I've spent many days and nights crying out to God for help and comfort, but it appears he had given up on me. It seemed like no matter how hard I prayed, I didn't receive an answer. I felt as if I was all alone and left in the dark. I wanted so much out of life.

I couldn't remember preparing a list of goals that included: to be pregnant, separated from my husband, and living in a financial mess. I never wanted any of that to happen to me. I thought my life would be prosperous and I believed the struggle would be light.

I started to believe everything that was happening was a mistake. I felt deep down inside God wouldn't give me more than I could bear. I knew God's Word was true. I asked God, "Why am I in such agony?" Yet God's timing to answer me was of His own power. I searched within myself and the answer was not there. I had my own feelings about why I was struggling. I felt that God had finally punished me for choosing my own path. The road I chose of sin led me down a path of struggle. I knew the choice was wrong, but I chose it anyway.

The feeling of our marriage ending began to reach my inner being. Brandon tuned me out financially as well as emotionally and the kids were the ones who would suffer.

He would give me twenty dollars here and there, yet I was paying twelve hundred dollars in bills by myself every month. Losing everything crossed my mind daily, as his help was desperately needed. According to Brandon, not communicating to me about money was his way of avoiding the whole situation.

The twenty dollars he gave me was plenty in his mind. For me to ask for more was out of the question. I became even more frustrated, leaving his place of work with tears streaming down my face. I could feel the anger rising on the inside of me like a boiling pot of water. I knew there had to be another way to get through to him.

With all the drama, I dealt with and the birth of our son; I had missed more than twelve weeks of work, which was more than my maternity time would cover. When I went back to work, my boss talked to me about the amount of time I missed from work.

She told me it was unacceptable and I didn't have any more days to miss or I would be terminated. Hearing those words, was like my boss had taken a knife and stabbed me in the stomach. I had never been terminated from any job before and it was certainly not an appropriate time for it to happen now.

I just knew I was dreaming and I would wake up to everything being ok. What I didn't know was that my maternity leave pay would hit me like a ton of bricks. What I received was not what I expected. I only had enough to cover one third of the bills. Yet, the landlord wanted all his money, cutting me no slack.

So, I began to pray, "*Lord, help me in this time of need. I don't have enough money to pay these people and they are telling me that I need to pay or get out. What am I to do? I don't want to lose my job either, but how am I going to pay these people? Help me to come up with something to get on the right track.*"

I prayed this prayer in hopes that God would hear me. Shortly after praying, my mother came over to my house. She began to say, "I know you are having a tough time right now, but I can't watch your kids or anybody's kids anymore. You are going to have to find someone to baby-sit as of today." I couldn't believe what I was hearing. There I was, praying to God for an answer, and bang! I got hit in the face with another load. It was Saturday and everything was closed. I was ready to pull all my hair out.

I stood there with tears in my eyes not knowing what to do. I knew that Brandon was not going to help me with the kids, but I had to check just in case I was wrong. I drove over to his house (his mother's house) as quickly as I could to ask him if he would watch the kids on Monday until I could figure out what to do about childcare.

Before he could say what, I knew he would say, I told him that I knew he had to work but I needed him to take a day off to watch the kids since I had missed so many days. I told Brandon that if I missed Monday, I would lose my job. He told me that he wasn't going to take the day off and that was that! I started to fuss and argue with him about not being responsible and how he put everything on me. He didn't seem to care. He refused to help me.

I went home trying to figure out what to do. I decided to call the emergency number that I had for my job and let them know that I would not be able to come to work on Monday.

Immediately my boss told me that I would be terminated. I decided that I didn't care anymore because my kids needed me more. I had to do what I had to do. I didn't know exactly what I was going to do, but I knew I had to do something.

Then it hit me. I realized that I could move before I got evicted. They told me that I could move or pay what was due. "Maybe I can beat the eviction, by moving first" I thought to myself. They did say I could move or pay. Little did I know, moving was still considered an eviction.

Yet, I decided to look for an apartment. Just when I was about to give up, a friend called and told me some good news. "All you need is ninety-nine dollars and you will be able to move into an apartment by me" she stated. I was excited. I went to the apartment and was approved the same day. I knew then that God heard me after all.

I decided to move the next day because I didn't have very much to move. I knew that I could do it all in one day. I left the house very excited that I was approved to get the key to my new apartment; I had no idea what was about to happen next. As soon as I pulled out to cross the street, a car coming directly my way hit me. I saw my whole life pass before my eyes. I just sat there in my car saying to myself, "this is a dream, I will wake up. Jesus, Jesus, spare me." I did wake up, and it wasn't a dream. People were running to the car to make sure I was okay and by the grace of God, no one was hurt! My car was damaged badly, but I was okay.

All I thought about was the fact that I wasn't dead. The events that took place in that week left me in disbelief for a moment that it happened. I slowly reviewed the things repeatedly in my mind of what had happened to me that week. It all seemed to kick off after I had just returned home from the hospital with my son. I was about to lose my job; I was about to be evicted; my mother was no longer able to keep the kids; I then lost my job; I searched for a new place to stay, and then to top it all off, I got in a car accident. I couldn't take anymore! I just knew that if one more thing was to happen to me, I would have gone crazy. Thank God! Nothing else happened to me that week.

I went on to move into my apartment by faith. I used the rental truck to complete my move that same day. The apartment that God blessed me with was about a thirty-minute drive away from family. I knew this would be a trying time for me and the kids.

Still separated from my husband meant having more lonely days to battle. Even though he hadn't been there for me, I still desired his love and comfort in the mist of my struggles. Yet I never received that comfort or love I desired. Instead the loneliness became heavy. I allowed my mind to sink its thoughts into my diary to ease the pressure. I prayed that God would hear my prayers once again.

November 14, 2002
"Dreams"

Dear Diary,

When you dream, you dream of being married and having a great big family in a lovely home living a happy life, but let's be realistic! Dreams come from within, a deep most inner thought and belief that no one can touch or alter; your dream is more precious than gold and more delicate than silk. The happiness you feel while having this dream is unreal, but very real to you. Dreams are something sacred that you share with someone that dreams as well. You can keep your dreams to yourself and hold on to them where you know they will be safe. When things are going bad around you, you can hide yourself in your dream and be as free as you want to be. There is no pain or heartache, you just dream.

I never wanted to stop dreaming. It appears being with Brandon destroyed my dreams. He wanted to make me what he thought I should be, even when he wasn't around. He was selfish with his love, and he didn't even want to let me know when he was ready to return home.

I waited and waited for Brandon to return home. Almost a year passed since he left and he still had me on a leash. He was holding on to my neck with his hands and I held onto him not letting him go either. I kept telling myself that he was just going through a phase and it would be over soon. I started to believe that my marriage was not anticipated at all. I thought Brandon wanted me to be the wife he married, but he just wanted a person to be with to do whatever he wanted to do, without the love, affection or responsibility of the family.

He finally decided to make his way over to my apartment, but only to get some sex whenever he wanted. I let him in and gave in to him thinking I would get the love and affection that I craved from him. I didn't. He told me that he was still thinking things over and wasn't ready to move back in yet.

The same excuse he gave me before. I gave him my body *again* and he still didn't want to move back in! How could he not be ready? I was busting my butt to take care of our family by myself, and he wasn't ready yet! I didn't understand him, nor did I want to believe that he wasn't ready. I knew he was playing games with my heart and only wanted me to tag along. He acted as if I didn't have a life.

November 17, 2002
"Some words to me"
3:01 A.M.

Dear Diary,

Sometimes I wonder what can be worse, feeling like you want your marriage, or not knowing if it is going to work. Here you are, battling deep feelings inside and you can't share them with anyone but yourself. On the other hand, you wish you could break out of this state of confusion and pain. You ask yourself, "What will the future hold?" and you answer yourself, "Only God knows." Why must it be this way? Is it supposed to be this way? Here you have a husband who doesn't know what he wants in life and doesn't' know how to express the love he has for his wife. He tells you the right things, but it doesn't come out in his actions like he said. Who's to blame? Is it life- the ages of male and female maturity; is it pride, or his self-conscience? I don't know what it is, but whatever it is, I hope it disappears. I want us to be able to express our emotions and I want our emotions lived out in our physical interactions. I must have a sense of feeling and understanding coming from my man; a sense of commitment and desire to satisfy my needs more than my wants. I need a man to support me in what I want to do with my time and future. I want to live a little, enjoy life and what it must offer. I want us to not be afraid to do some things a little different from normal or average; I want him to listen to what I must say and not just hear what I am saying. That is very important! Communication is the number one thing we need in this marriage. I want him to get inside of me (feel) me and know me! When he gets inside my head and soul, I will know, because he will understand why things are broken down when having a conversation; he will understand why I need feedback and opinion. These are just a few. I need to hear sweet things in my ear; he needs to say how much he cares for me. If there is no romance, then the love can die. If you never tell a person that you love them, then doubt begins to rise in the thoughts and arguments will breakout. The more good signals we send to one another, the better we will get along! There should be deep, passionate love making that is supposed to bring you closer as a husband and a wife.

The more I wanted Brandon the less of him I got. He came around like a distant friend. I just couldn't believe how I let him control my life, even when he wasn't with me. I just didn't know how to let go of him in my heart. I wanted so much at that time in my life. The thing I most hungered for was the love of my man and he didn't give it to me! He used to say the words "I love you," later I had to ask if he even cared.

How did we get to the point where he held everything against me? I couldn't even be myself without him being mad. I couldn't tell him how much I loved him without him telling me what I did to him. I couldn't dare ask him to spend time with his children, without him telling me that I was the one who wanted them.

What do you tell someone like that? I just couldn't keep quiet! That was not me. I refused to let him hold me in a pattern of silence and expect me to love without wanting it in return.

I began to think on more important things other than the fact that my love life was ruined. I reminded myself that time was running out for me to find a job that would pay the bills. I went on the hunt and came up with nothing; only to realize that if I didn't get daycare for the kids, I wouldn't be able to work.

So, I did the only thing I knew how to and that was to find where I could get such help. As time went on searching at the career center, it sent me nowhere but it did give me a two-year stretch on daycare. I decided to go where I was familiar, back to the fast food life. I worked in fast food for four years when I was in high school and unfortunately, they didn't treat me right then.

I knew they wouldn't treat me right if I went back, but I needed the money to pay the bills. I worked there for two months and moved on to another job paying just as little for two more months.

I just couldn't seem to help myself and I felt helpless. My brother needed a place to stay so I thought that this would be an effective way to help me out of the rut I was in. We both had our own problems, but we thought that maybe we could stick together and things would work out. I had not realized that living with my brother would be so different from when we were kids. I had my own way of living, and he had his. We both didn't fit together under the same roof.

While the differences of our living situation came to the surface, I began to feel my emotions battling inside of me screaming to be heard.

November 18, 2002
8:28 P.M.

Dear Diary, I am just a leaky pipe dripping continuously without ceasing. I'll travel as far as the sea and hide beneath the pier. Drifting farther and farther away from the land I once knew; to hide myself from the pain and suffering that I must endure. There's no stopping me; there's no compromise, only the safety of being in peace will I allow; a place where I can rest and capture my thoughts; a place of inner peace and spiritual relaxation; a place of no strain and strife; a place where arguments don't exist. It doesn't have to be a place of riches or gold, because there's no need for money, fashion, or fame. All you need to go to this wonderful place is your imagination; the place of no strain. To be like the sun would be such an experience, to rise in the east and set in the west. To be all over the world in so many places at once. Oh, how I long for the freedom.

The more alone I felt, the more I had to write to get what I felt off my chest. I tried calling Brandon to tell him just how I felt, but my words were shambled and I was the only one talking. He would sit silently on the phone and all I would hear was his breathing coming from his end of the phone. I couldn't tell my brother what I was feeling because he didn't even understand what he was feeling. I couldn't tell anyone. I was alone, alone with my pain. I didn't know how much of the pain I would be able to take. All I wanted was to be out of debt, take care of my family, and have someone to love me. If only life was that easy!

I cried and prayed that God would take the pain away and give me peace. I just couldn't turn my back on God. I knew that even though I was not receiving the answers that I wanted, God was still there. God was waiting to give me all the gifts that he had in store for me, I just didn't know when.

I wanted to get back with my husband sooner than later. I gave our separation a time limit- exactly one year from the day we separated. If Brandon was not ready to be a couple by May 2003, I told myself, I would walk away from the marriage and divorce him. I just couldn't bear to wait another year, month, or day for someone who didn't want me.

I wrote:

1. When coming back together from a long separation there should be change. Things should not be the same as they were before.

2. There must be counseling to get an understanding of each other and marriage.

3. There should be rules on how to not make the same mistakes again.

4. There should be commitment to take care of responsibilities. Each should take into consideration what the other had to endure over the separation. If there are kids, the other person needs to know what the other had to do to take care of the kids alone and what sacrifices were made.

5. Both should come together to support one another. Without support, it is very hard to show the other person that you care about what he/she does and wants.

6. Support comes into play when one wants to do something that will benefit the family. Always listen to each other before making a judgment. If you don't agree with what the person wants, then ask various questions such as: why do you want this? What will this do for you if you have it? How would this affect you if you don't have it?

7. Tell the other person how you feel. Don't tell the other person that they can't do something. Don't threaten them. Threatening will cause an argument.

8. Sometimes you must let your mate make their mistakes for them to recognize the wrong.

CHAPTER 5

THE BETRAYAL
OF LONELINESS

The more I was alone, the more it hurt for me to think about it. I just wanted to be happy and full of life. I was changing before my eyes. The desire to enjoy life and what it had to offer was no longer a priority. I just wanted to survive in this world of cruelty and its unkindness. The world had given me the person I chose, but not what I wanted at all.

It seems funny how the world works and how the cycle of life depends upon the choices we make. If we make the wrong choices in life, we will reap the consequences of those choices.

If we choose the man or woman that God had not given to us to be our companion, we can be cursed and only God can bring us out. We must choose God first, and then allow him to lead you to make the right choices from that day forward. We try to choose right from wrong and stay on the right path without God. Why do you think that is?

All the signs were there in front of me that Brandon was not the man for me, yet I couldn't resist the desires of my flesh. The human nature of wanting to be loved and to feel the compassion from someone special is what I allowed to control me. I wanted to give what I had inside of me, to give my true self. I did just that. I gave all of me and didn't get what I craved in return.

Even though time had passed, there was still hunger inside of me to love him. I knew that Brandon probably wouldn't change, but maybe, just maybe, there was a way that he could. I believed that God could give a miracle if I prayed hard enough for him to. I wanted my marriage more and more. At the same time, was it wrong for me to want to be free of him?

I sat, every day in the apartment, feeling alone. I had my children, but I still felt alone.

I wanted some type of assurance that Brandon loved me and a reason why I he acted as if he didn't love me too. I started to feel that the love he once had for me left.

I called him up one day and all he told me was that he needed six more months to think things over because he felt pressured. I didn't want to pressure him, but he didn't know how much my heart ached for him. I felt that I was on an emotional rollercoaster and I had flown to Mars. Maybe he thought things were supposed to fall back together again magically. I knew it didn't work that way. I felt that there was such a hole in the relationship to the point where all I felt, was the emptiness.

December 1, 2002
12:30 A.M.

Dear Diary,

I am hurting very much inside because I am crying out for love and answers. I don't understand why Brandon would push me away because he's confused. He says he doesn't understand me. He says I am like night and day and he doesn't know if he loves me. He also goes on to say that we have these big arguments and he's all confused. He tells me to go ahead and get my divorce. I asked him "why?" He gives me the same reason that he doesn't know how long it would take for him to understand me. I couldn't believe he was saying all of this after the length of time I have waited. I have given myself to him, yet I still didn't get anywhere with him. "Maybe I will have to just get him out of my system the best way I know how, by finding another companion." I thought to myself.

As the rage ran through my blood, I began to see nothing but revenge. I wanted to hurt him the way he had hurt me and I wanted to make him feel the pain. I wanted him to feel all the loneliness and heartache of wanting someone that he couldn't have. I thought about how I was going to pull it off, and then it came to me.

A childhood crush would do. I had talked to my childhood crush and now the tables were turned. He had a crush on me. He was the perfect choice to use in this horrible act. I had never been with anyone other than my husband, but I desired my friend to give me what I had been craving so long, "love and affection."

His name was Andrew Boston. I had a crush on him when I was just fourteen years old. He was the sweetest person, but lived so far away. I wanted to be his girlfriend back then, but he was three years older than me and I knew he didn't want to give me a chance.

So, I never told him. I couldn't believe he had moved to my location. The shoe was on the other foot! He looks me up and comes over to my house to catch up.

Then he gives me hints that he's interested. I told him that I was going to get back with Brandon, but he didn't seem to care and continued to pursue me. Andrew came over one night and we talked as usual. I just couldn't bring myself to tell him that Brandon wanted me to go ahead and divorce him.

Deep inside, I still wanted Brandon. I knew deep down inside that Andrew and I could never be. I just wanted to experience what it might feel like to be held after making love and what it felt like to look at someone in the eyes and share some sort of a feeling.

I decided to make my move even though I felt it might not work. I told Andrew that I wanted him to stay the night and he happily accepted. We played around for a while and my heart literally raced in my chest. At the same time, I was asking myself what in the world was I doing?

As I laid with Andrew and him on me, then in me, I began to feel sick inside. I felt no pleasure whatsoever. I had never been so low, doing something so wrong. I felt that maybe I would be able to release the hurt and pain that I felt. When he was done, I felt no relief.

There was no magic in the air. I didn't feel that he had swept me off my feet or made me feel complete. I didn't feel refreshed or revised, but still hungry for affection.

I wanted to tell him my painful secret that I was just using him. Then I heard his phone ring softly, he answered and not to my surprise, a girl. I knew then that he had used me too. We both decided to never again speak to one another about the day we used each other.

I felt as if I had dipped my soul deeper into the pits of hell. I knew that I was condemning myself with the act. I just hoped and prayed that he would one day forgive me. I stayed to myself after that event took place. I didn't call Brandon, nor did I call Andrew. I knew that I was still battling the feelings that I had for Brandon that didn't go away with my actions.

I couldn't help but pray: *Lord, forgive me. What I did was wrong and I still have love for Brandon with all my heart and you know that. I am asking you to ease the pain as I end my marriage that I longed for, for so long. Please forgive me for going ahead of your will and doing it my way without letting you do it. Lord, I ask that you please help me be strong and hold my head up, for there's a reason for this season. Please Lord; help me be the one you want me to be. Take me down the golden path that you have prepared for me to take. Take me by the hand and hold me until I walk strong. Let me lean not to my own understanding, and don't let me drift away into the sea of forgetfulness. Let me be a strong tower that rises over every nation, and let me sing the songs of Zion and praise your name for I want to come out of the wilderness with the victory. I have endured the hardship of hardships. I will have won the battle and I will fight until I die, and when there is no one around to lean on, I will stand. For when there is no ground for any more battle I will stand, I will stand. Amen.*

Time didn't seem to wait for my heart to catch up; it just passed me by before I even knew it. I was entering a new year with my eyes still closed, hoping that God had an answer for me about the entire struggle I endured over the last year. I felt like the world was against everything and nothing seemed to go in the right direction. I needed some guidance and some type of direction that would lead me on the way to freedom.

I was at the breaking point of my life and I didn't know if I was coming or going. It was February and approaching the year mark of our separation. I was still debating whether to give Brandon the time or take the divorce road. I wasn't happy at all. As a matter of fact, I couldn't remember the last time I was happy.

During this time, I became frustrated a lot. I would sit in my two-bedroom apartment with my brother annoyed that we could not blend our way of living. I sat in front of the T.V. wishing that a miracle would come my way and erase all the stress and pain I felt. It felt as if bills were rolling in by the minute and my income taxes were stuck in the previous year. I couldn't even get rapid refund because my credit was so bad. Money seemed to mysteriously disappear.

Three hundred and twenty dollars came up missing out of my wallet and my brother seemed not to know what happened to it.

I just wanted a piece of mind. I was contemplating ending my marriage and praying that God had a plan for me. God knew I loved my kids and the life he had allowed me to live, but the load that I was carrying was unbearable.

I spent a year going through emotional pain, rejection, and debt. I didn't know how much more I could take! A year was too long for me to go through something alone. I was tired of being tired.

I finally talked to Brandon after a month to myself. I took some time to think about what I was going to do about the divorce. He told me that he was having second thoughts, but still wanted me to wait it out to see what he felt later.

He kept tugging at my heart, telling me one thing, and then changing it just to keep me in his loop. I sometimes felt that I owed him for stepping out on him with us still being married. I did wonder whom he was with because I knew he wasn't keeping to himself as much as he loved sex. He wouldn't go three days without sex; I knew he didn't go months without it!

During this time, my mother called to tell me that she was moving out of her one-bedroom apartment. She told me that I could take over the lease if I wanted it. She said the rent was much cheaper and the utilities were included so it would be less strain on me. I told her it would be a wonderful idea since my brother and I did not see eye to eye. I told my brother that he could take over my lease and have the apartment. I knew it would be great for me to start over and be somewhere without stress.

I moved that same weekend and made sure that all the bills that I had to take care of were handled. I felt relieved as I started out again in faith. I knew that my job wasn't going to hold up, but I didn't give up on looking for a new one to start the year.

I still wasn't solid on my decision about my marriage. I decided to tell Brandon anyway that I was done and we should get a divorce soon. I didn't have the money then to do it and I wasn't about to ask Brandon. I wanted so much more than to worry about the expenses of a divorce and how I was going to feed my kids, yet I was willing to end it all to ease my heart ache.

I decided to go to Brandon's house to tell him that the best thing for us was to call it quits. He wanted to spend more time with his friends and never any time with his family. This was my first time ever telling him I wanted to end it after an entire year. I felt this was the best decision I could think of. What I didn't imagine was that he would play the beg card on me.

One Friday night about nine o' clock, I walked up to Brandon's door. As I walked up to the door, I could hear his voice inside before I rang the doorbell. I took a deep breath before telling him what I dreaded so long.

He opened the door with the look of surprise. I quickly told him that I needed to speak to him for a minute. He took a deep breath knowing that whatever I had to say was serious and he probably didn't want to hear it. After my second-deep breath, I just let it flow, "I want a divorce." I waited for a response but he just looked at me as if his entire world had come crashing down all at once.

"A divorce why?" He said with a stutter. "What do you mean why? You were the one that said go ahead with my life and you didn't want to hold me back because I was rushing you." I reminded him. He just stood there in awe, wishing he could take back his words.

I reminded him that not only had he been avoiding the boys, he didn't have time for me. I went on to say that I just wanted to be happy and couldn't wait for him any longer. As I walked away, he grabbed my arm gently saying, "Please don't go, I want to talk to you." I turned quickly and told him that there was nothing else to talk about. I started to walk again and he began to beg me not to leave and let him talk. I just shook my head and told him no. I wanted to run as fast as I could, but my legs wouldn't move.

I walked slowly to my car wishing that Brandon would stop begging me to talk to him. As I reached my car, he was still behind me. He asked me to let him come to my apartment and discuss the situation.

The first thing that came to mind was sex. All he wanted from me was sex. I knew he wanted my body and not my mind. Yet he kept on saying he had changed and gave his life over to the Lord and that he just needed another chance.

I still felt as if I owed him another chance and deep down I wanted my marriage just as bad as he claimed he did. I finally gave in to his horrible begging and took him to my apartment. The kids were with my mother for the weekend. I was happy to not show my stress around the children and have a little time to myself, I thought. When we arrived at my home, I knew things might not go as smoothly as I hoped. I didn't know what to expect really. It had been so long since we had spoken.

We started talking and he didn't waste any time telling me how he changed. He told me what he was going to do for the family if I gave him a second chance. I was hearing him, but at the same time, I was praying that he meant every word. I didn't want to go through the same pain that I had endured for so long.

Then he did it. He asked me what I feared he would. "Have you been with anyone else?" "Have you?" I quickly asked. Then he went on to tell me this whole story about some girl and claimed it happened in high school. I knew the story wasn't truthful because it didn't add up. I decided to go ahead and tell him about Andrew and the reason I did it. He began to make faces as if he was crying, yet not tears. All I could think of was how phony he was. I knew deep down inside that he was angry and wanted revenge.

As soon as we had our deep discussion, he wanted to have sex. I figured. I told him that I didn't want to. He acted as if he needed to be comforted, but he really wanted to reclaim my body. I decided to let him comfort himself but redeeming himself was what he really wanted to do. I sunk right back into the sad state I was in.

He hurt me that night, physically and emotionally. I was so weak for him I allowed it. I later tried to explain to him just how he hurt me but he didn't want to hear it.

He quickly changed back to his old ways and I had already agreed to let him move in. I wished I had the strength to tell him no, but I didn't. I sunk right back into his trap and he had me just where he wanted me, with him. For the next three months, my job went downhill. I began to worry about how I was going to tell him that he was the one that would have to bring home the income.

I told Brandon that a guy at my job was hitting on me and I didn't want to work there anymore. I knew with his jealousy he would fall right for it. He quickly told me that I didn't have to and could look for another job. He said that he would hold everything up.

I could handle myself when it came to any guy flirting with me, yet I just knew if I told him that I and some other employees were lied to about our pay and how after taxes it wasn't worth working there. I just knew he would have blown another gasket about me not doing what I suppose to do. He wouldn't have cared about the facts, just the difference he would have to pay in bills. I needed a way to get him to pull the slack for me and the kids until I could. For I knew it was just a matter of time before he wouldn't.

April rolled around and I still couldn't seem to find a job. My car payment was behind and Brandon refused to pay the car note for me. He also refused to pay the insurance and so the bills for the car were left unpaid. I knew it was a matter of time before "they" came to get the car.

I decided to go downtown and look for a job and just my luck, lost the car keys and couldn't get a replacement set. The car was stuck on the side of the road collecting tickets and I couldn't do anything about it, but cry. I had to get a ride home because Brandon was working and wouldn't come get me. He told me that it was my fault that I was in that situation because I didn't have a job.

I just couldn't believe he was blaming me for everything that I had no control over. I couldn't take the kids to daycare, and he refused. I couldn't find a job close to home, and he blamed me.

Then a knock on the door; "Hello, can I help you?" I asked the gentleman standing outside the door, as I peeked through the peephole. "I am sorry ma'am, but I am here to collect your debt owed for the amount on the car, and I need all of the money now, or the car." I opened the door to finally talk to the man behind the demand.

I quickly told the man that the car was impounded and that he would have to get it from the pound. He thanked me and left. When Brandon returned from work, I told him what happened and he wasn't supportive at all. He reminded me that I was without a job and told me that he was tired of paying all the bills. He had a lot of nerves, "Ha! I paid ninety-five percent of the bills by myself for three years!" We argued about the whole subject and I was fed up with his irresponsibility, yet I felt I couldn't do anything about it.

July 21, 2003
3:31 P.M.

Dear Diary,

I have been stuck in this house for four months and the arguments just won't stop. All Brandon does now is bicker that his car had broken down. I have been stuck in this apartment without any transportation; I had to walk to the store with two children and carry the heavy groceries up three flights of stairs all by myself. Brandon wouldn't take us anywhere and we can't walk anywhere else, because everything is too far away. I just hate that I ever gave him a second chance, now I am stuck. My brother has now given me a little car to get from point A to point B and Brandon wants to use my car for his pleasure. I said no, because he is not going to treat me bad with his car and then expect me to be his servant when he needs one. I told him things might go a little better for him if he starts treating the kids and me better. I now must drive him back and forth to work for us to have money for the bills. He gives me a little to pay a certain bill, and then he wants it back to buy whatever he doesn't need. Then he gets mad about me asking him for gas, and daycare money, because this is what he knew I needed to get a job. I better not say I am sick. Yesterday and today I had been sick. He treated me like crap. First, he says I'm not that sick and I am dead to the world if I am sick. So, when I needed him to get off from work, he tells me he can't and I need to stop acting like I can't handle anything when I am sick. When he does get home, he wouldn't watch the kids while I lay in bed to recover. Oh, and don't think he offers me any food or water. Then he turns around and says,

"Since you can't handle anything while you're sick I won't give you the bill money anymore until I feel I'm ready to." I know he's tired of paying all the bills for the last three months, because he has complained about it every other day. I feel he should just quit and go live under a box. All he does is nag that he never has any time for himself; he doesn't have a car, complain, and complain. He has never once thanked me for washing his clothes, cooking his food, taking care of the kids and babying him when he is sick; giving him all the sex he craves, and not complaining in his face. He should try doing everything I have done; going to work and coming home to do it all over again for three years straight without complaining, then maybe I will rub him on his back. I would love to give him the credit if he was taking care of his family willingly, because he is the man and loves us just that much. He has let me know that he doesn't like doing this job as a man or a husband. He has a circle that goes around his head and it has Brandon in the middle with a lot of Brandon's around him with his friends' right behind him following his every move. Yet his family is as far away from him as possible. I feel like I am just in his life trying to be seen by him and all he does is step on me. Soon I am going to disappear and there will be nothing left of me. He better starts realizing what he has because it can be gone before he knows what hit him.

CHAPTER 6

A CRY FOR CHANGE

I continued to tell myself that things would change and all I had to do was keep the faith and not let Brandon get me in the dumps. I still had a prayer inside of me that Brandon would change and maybe our marriage would survive.

We continued to live in our apartment that my mom left me. She told me that the apartment was in my sister's name and I was responsible for making sure I paid the rent on time. I had no problem with getting the rent in on time; I just had the problem with getting the money from Brandon to make sure the rent was paid.

The rent was five hundred and fifty dollars and the utilities were included. Even though the rent was affordable, the one-bedroom apartment seemed to have gotten too cluttered for the four of us. Once Brandon moved all his things in, the apartment looked like a Cracker Jack box. I just couldn't keep the mess off the floors and the clutter out of the way. I knew that we could find something bigger for the four of us to live in.

I became frustrated with not only the apartment, but with the responsibility that fell on my plate. I had so many clothes to wash that I just couldn't wash all of them at the same time. We lived on the third floor of the apartment complex and the washing machines were located on the first floor.

They were either broken or unavailable. I couldn't leave the clothes down stairs unattended because someone would take them. I carried the children, one on my hip and the other walking, to wash over seven loads of clothes at the laundry mat. Not only did the kids dirty their clothes, but Brandon acted as if he was a super model, changing close often. I washed and folded the clothes and then carried them up three flights of stairs alone. I didn't get any help from Brandon, who claimed he was working.

I began to estimate his hours of work. I added up the time he spent away from home including the amount of time he spent at home. He began to spend less and less time at home and more time in the streets again. I wanted to know what he was doing four hours after work.

He couldn't give me a straight answer. All he would say was he was looking for another job because I had been out of work for so long. I told him that was great, but the least he could have done was to call and let me know he was safe and check on us. I was home cooking and cleaning the house for him and he would come home around eight in the evening when the dinner was cold and the kids were in the bed.

I only could imagine what he really was doing. I didn't trust him as far as I could throw him. Every time I asked him something he would tell a lie to cover whatever lie he told before. When I found out that he told me a lie, he would still deny the lie even more. The anger inside of me began to build and all I could see was this so-called man that couldn't and wouldn't tell me the truth.

All I wanted was the truth. I wanted to know that we could have trust in our relationship and that we could be open with one another about anything. Unfortunately, it was the other way around. The mistrust, the lies, and deceit were all there.

I realized that after I confessed my sins of betrayal to Brandon he was out to get me back in whatever way he knew how.

He decided to resent me and call me out of my name as much as possible. I just didn't realize the depth of his anger and how he wanted me to be as miserable as he felt. He pretended some days to be happy. When he wanted my attention in a sexual way he was happy. He changed right after that. I was deceived in so many ways.

Brandon continued to throw my wrongs in my face. He told me that I was still cheating on him and he didn't care if I never got another job. He went on to say that if I did get another job, I needed to make sure that there were no men in the building because he didn't trust me around any man.

I immediately told him that I was not going to be his Jinni in a bottle anymore like I had been for the past four months. I told Brandon that I was going to get a job and I didn't care if there were men in the building. I felt he had lost his mind and I refused to wait around any longer.

I got up the next day and applied for a job. I remembered that I knew a customer from my old job that was a manager, so I took the opportunity to ask him for a job. He told me that he had just the right opening for me and if I wanted it, I could have it. I happily accepted the job. It was my opportunity to redeem myself and bring in the money that I knew could help us. I wanted to move out of the small apartment we were living in. So, to do just that, a budget had to be created.

When I arrived home, I told Brandon I got a job, "About time. Now I don't have to give you all the money; you can pay half and I can pay half of the bills." He said. "Half" I responded. "We are married, there shouldn't be a half.

How can you sit here and try to split things up when I don't even have a check yet?" He responded by telling me that he had been paying the bills all this time and he was no longer going to use all his money just for bills.

I couldn't believe what my ears were hearing and to think that he was the one taking care of us. I wanted to hit him up side his head and tell him to leave and I would take care of the kids and myself. I could sense that he did give up the money unwillingly, but it got us to where we were.

I waited until the next week to bring up the fact that I still wanted a better apartment. I needed Brandon's help with looking for a new place and decided to pay the down payment. Brandon kept telling me we didn't have to move and we were fine where we were.

We argued about the topic of moving almost every day until he realized that I wasn't going to give up on getting a bigger place. I looked in newspapers and came across a nice two-bedroom apartment for six-hundred-dollars a month. I called the landlord immediately to set up some type of payment arrangement to hold the apartment for us.

I was excited that we were in God's favor. We had to pay the rest of the month's rent before we could move, but at the same time, we only had to pay two hundred dollars for the first month's rent for the new apartment.

The months couldn't seem to go fast enough. Brandon finally got the second job he was looking for. He then told me that he was going to quit the old job and keep the new job. I told him, if that's what he wanted to do I was completely fine with it. I wanted him to make sure that his new job was what he really wanted. He told me it was and not to worry about him, because he would be fine.

The nights began to grow longer before Brandon reached home in a decent hour. His work hours were from nine A.M. to five P.M. and he still didn't return home until 9p.m. or later. I didn't understand why he wanted to continue to stay away from home, or why he wanted to continue to deceive me. He did not care to pick up the phone and call me and let me know he was still alive. I couldn't put my finger on it.

So, I waited up for him to come home one night and I asked him about it. We argued the same tune repeatedly about how he was grown and how he could do what he wanted to. Yet, I was supposed to do my wifely duties and tend to the house, the kids and him.

One cold November night I waited up for Brandon to make sure he came in safely and all he wanted to do was fuss. The baby wasn't feeling well and I wasn't in the mood to argue, like I am ever. I told myself that maybe; just maybe, if I keep my mouth shut, he wouldn't continue to nag to me. I was wrong. The more I didn't say anything, the angrier he became. He started irritating me by poking me and telling me that neither one of us was going to go to sleep that night unless I talked to him. I still refused to say anything but, "leave me alone." I left the living room and went into the bedroom locking him out.

He banged and picked at the door, but couldn't get it open. He went as far as to take off the doorknob, but still couldn't get in. I couldn't believe that he was so angry about nothing. He just wouldn't stop.

The babies were at the point of waking up from all the noise, so I opened the door. He immediately grabbed me by the leg and dragged me out of the room. I was kicking and yelling at him to let me go. He told me that I was going to talk to him no matter what. I finally pushed him off me and I told him that he was crazy and that I would rather sleep in the car, than to be in the same house with him. I got up, grabbed the keys to my car, and opened the door. I had to run down three flights of stairs hoping he wouldn't follow.

I jumped in my car locking the doors behind me. I was so happy to see that he wasn't behind me. I finally had peace. I turned on the car to receive some heat and laid the seat back to look at the moon. It was a full moon that night.

I stared at it and wished that I could disappear. I wanted so desperately to run to someone and tell anyone everything that happened. I couldn't get up enough strength to share my problems with anyone. I decided to stay in my warm car for two hours just to rest a while. Once I got back upstairs, he had gone to sleep. I was once again at peace.

Even though I wanted Brandon home in the evenings, I really didn't want him there. I wanted the peace of him being in my presence, but when he was, there just wasn't any peace. I knew that I had to forgive him once again about what he did to me that night, but I knew I would not forget it.

The hurt swelled up in me and turned more and more into hatred and despise. I wanted a divorce every time I looked at him. My mind told me that the happiness I longed for wasn't close to me and it didn't look like I would ever have it.

January of 2004 finally arrived and we moved into our new apartment. I thought that maybe it would be a little less stressful. I wanted more and more in life. As the years seemed to fly by, I visualized myself going back to school and furthering my education. I wanted to become more valuable at work and go up the prosperity ladder instead of down the debt hill.

January 20, 2004
Words to my husband

Dear Diary,

Time has passed. So, how much time do you think it will take before you claim me as your wife and your family as your family? Let's just cut it short; do you love me? Not just enough to stand by me, but enough to claim me as your wife, to honor me with those words you promised at the altar. You should want to drop the past and move toward a new beginning.

Do you love me enough to give me what I deserve?
Which is: true love, respect, forgiveness, honesty, kindness,
responsibility, sincerity, compassion, communication, a Godly
conscience, and support?

    I want you to treat me like a lady. Make me feel like I am
wanted and loved. Make me number one over all. Support me
and don't bring me down. If you want this marriage tell me
now, if not then we will let it go. How long does it take to tell
that someone you love, has love for you? How long does it take
to express your true feelings and mean it? How much longer;
another year; six months? How long should I have to wait to
have the good man that I know you can be? Should I have to
wait if the love is already there? What am I waiting for, is it
true love? I can't and won't wait another year with you to feel
loved. I love you enough to let you go. When I do let you go, I
will never return. If you won't change the way you live now and
become this man that you say you are, then you never will and
you really don't love me. If we can't put God first in our
marriage then it will not work and it will fall apart. If all that
comes to mind is hate and anger, then you are still stuck in the
past and the past will consume you. If you want to hold a
contest on who has the most baggage then you can't even begin
to count mine, because I would win between the hurt and the
pain that I carry every day. I am getting tired of running behind
this marriage and you. So, if you don't change, then I will have
to change the whole marriage world for you.

    It seemed like the more I wanted to express myself, the more
Brandon didn't understand me. The more I tried to tell him my
goals and desires, the less he wanted a goal or desire. He began
to get comfortable with his surroundings and the way he was
living his life. I always stressed that I felt held back from making

my life what I wanted it to be. You can live in a world and never really live. Life is truly what you make it. I felt that Brandon was just around and not really living life to the fullest. I felt like he was pulling me with him.

I wanted to fulfill my dreams and fill my life with endless beauty. I wanted to enjoy life and what it had to offer. I decided that just dreaming wasn't going to change my future and talking about it wasn't going to make anything come to pass. I took the challenge to enroll myself in college and start from there.

I confronted my husband about being supportive of me, but he wasn't. He told me that we were adults and we didn't have time or the money to worry about college. So, I went and enrolled myself into college on my own, hoping that maybe one day I would win his support in the long run.

Going to school twice a week, on top of everything else was becoming a big load for me to carry. When I asked Brandon for a little help with the kids and bills, I didn't get it. I became unhappy with the way things were at home.

It seemed all he wanted to do was work and stay out with his friends. I was the one that was supposed to do everything. I began to nag about taking his role as a father and how he instead acted as a stranger to the family. I asked him if he would just work with me as a husband and wife team, but he seemed to not understand where I was coming from.

The more I nagged, the more he resented me, and the more I resented him. We became distant in our own home. I just wanted change.

He told me that he just wanted me to leave him alone. I just couldn't seem to leave things alone when he lied to me about his pay, and the bills were not getting paid. I didn't understand why he didn't want to talk to me and be more of my companion. I didn't know what else to do but nag.

All I wanted to do was communicate to him the things that were most important. Such as: the kids, bills and spending time together. He would get angry every time I brought up the subjects.

He told me he didn't want to talk about it right then and to leave it alone and we would talk about it later. I would wait days to bring up the issues again and he would get even more upset.

My mind went in circles trying to communicate with Brandon. As soon as I told myself to close my mouth and not nag, then he would act as if he had been cool all along and I was the one with the attitude.

We never saw eye to eye and each of us wanted things to be our way. I had totally different thoughts and he had different views. I wanted our marriage to be based on being one mind and one soul. We were unequally yoked and everything we did or said fell apart at the seams.

I began to feel more and more lost. I did not understand myself anymore. I started to feel that being with Brandon was only bringing me down and I just needed to separate myself from him. I wanted to get away from him and escape. I reminded him that we never went to counseling and maybe we should go before I lost my mind.

He agreed. When we got there, I just sat there and listened to him tell the Pastor how he was going to change and work with me better in the marriage. I told the Pastor that I was unsure about what Brandon said but was willing to stop nagging so much and give him a chance to change.

He went to church with me twice in one week to show his efforts. The following week, when the money fell short, we were at each other's throats again.

We fussed and fussed about the bills and how they would be paid. We just couldn't come to an agreement on how things should be operated. I decided to ease my brain by writing in my journal every day and document the daily events to see where the problems were.

July 30, 2004
6:14 P.M.
Pay Day

Dear Diary,
Today is payday and that means bill day for me. The morning started out about 4 A.M. and I noticed that Brandon already had an attitude and acted as if he didn't want anything to do with me. We both went back to sleep and I got up about six A.M. to take the unwanted dog out that I got from a coworker for the kids since we got rid of the last dog. When I got back in, I noticed that Brandon was already dressed and ready to go to work but the babies were not. It was six-thirty A.M. and he didn't have to be to work until eight A.M. so I asked him why he was leaving so early. He quickly said that he needed to go check on his mother. I thought to myself that he just was over there yesterday and his mother was not sick. So why was he doing this? I had to be at work at seven A.M. I still had to dress the kids, drop the kids at day care, and get there on time. It didn't happen. I was late getting to work. I worked my butt off all day thinking about getting these bills paid and moving on. I got off work, paid our car insurance, and went to Brandon's job to get the rest of the money for the bills. He would usually get the money during lunch but today he tells me that he didn't go and he was going to the bank after work. After telling me that, he then questioned me about the bills and told me that he wanted to split his half in another half because he wasn't going to have his amount. I quickly told him, "No, that would not be right." I

only had enough for the certain bills, and now he wants me to pay even more. I left so upset and I knew that there was nothing I could do about him not giving me the money. I thought that I would come home and have at least one night without stress and worry, but I was stressed out to the point of no return.

It seemed that my mind was running away from me. The only person that knew was not a person at all but "my diary." I didn't know how much more I could take. All I knew was that I was tired and wasn't getting through to Brandon in any way. The more I needed his help, the more things seemed to change around me.

I received notice at work that one of the managers was quitting. That meant that I had to work two nights a week to cover the shifts. I mentioned the change to Brandon. He immediately reminded me that he got off work at six P.M. and would not be able to pick the kids up.

I tried to give him different options but he was trying not to hear me. I decided to ask my mother to help me with the kids. She told me that she could pick them up some nights but not all.

Asking Brandon's Aunt or Uncle was out of the question, for he would have acted like I wanted to pull their teeth. I had to figure out a way to get the kids home before my shift started or simply leave work, get them, and then go back to work.

To make matters worse, I found out that the kids' health insurance was canceled. I had to make an appointment and miss work to get things straight. The bullets kept coming. I had no help from Brandon.

He told me that he burned his pay stubs and didn't have any to give me for proof of income for the kids' insurance. That made my brain boil and I knew that I had to wait a month or two to get our kids some type of insurance.

I continued to go to work at night and it seemed like the more I did at work, the longer the nights became. I came home from work tired many nights, and all I had to show for it was a cut in hours. I just couldn't seem to win for losing and the stress was not going away. I thought about putting in my two weeks' notice and finding another job before I killed myself working for a company that did not appreciate me. I wanted to become salaried, but they kept telling me I needed to work at least sixty hours a week and not have any kids. I knew that was discrimination.

There was no way I would work sixty hours a week for ten-seventy an hour and neglect my kids anyway! I just wanted my normal thirty-hours a week but they cut me down to twenty hours. That wasn't enough for the bills and daycare.

It seemed like the more I tried to get ahead, the further away I got. I wanted to finish at least one project in my life and have some success doing so. I continued to go to school twice a week and go to work. I went home wishing on a star that things would change. The more nights I worked, the less time I had to argue with Brandon. I felt relieved in a sense.

I wanted to see the good in Brandon and what he had to offer the family, but I couldn't see it. If I asked him to clean, he would pick two items up off the floor and complain about it.

Nothing he did anymore was heartfelt. I felt like the load was getting too heavy for me and I didn't know how much longer I could hold it. I consulted with my diary to see if I was insensitive. I felt as if I was a detective trying to solve an investigation and the case was not being solved fast enough.

Time was ticking and my stress level was almost to the roof. It seemed like no matter what I said to him, I would strike a nerve. I wanted to get things taken care of and he didn't help. I wanted to make life as easy as possible by doing the necessary things for the family. The kids' birthdays would come and go and Brandon was not a part of the activities. I just didn't know how to reach out to Brandon and get through to him. I started to feel like a castaway.

I look back at what we both were trying to do in our marriage. I realized that we both had dreams or idea that didn't include each other.

Brandon came to me and told me that he wanted to be a rapper. He said that he was going to make it happen with or without me. I told him that was fine and that he needed to get his priorities straight with his family first.

All he wanted to do was spend more and more time with his high school boys. I never got a chance to get a break from the kids to just breathe or rest. I wanted to have a little peace for once without all the bickering, but it didn't seem as though I would get it. I managed to hold my tongue and not say too much to him when he became upset, but the cold shoulder and no talking seemed to get to him more. He would walk around the house with an attitude. He told me that I was the one with the problem or attitude and just like that, we were back at it.

I was running out of solutions to solve the argument problems that we had. I asked him again about counseling and the answer was still, "No." I decided to talk to my Pastor on my own and let him know what the problem was. I desperately wanted to live in a happy and peaceful environment, but my mind was going in circles.

I went to church to the next meeting with the Pastor and mentioned to him that, no matter how I put it, Brandon really didn't want counseling. The Pastor said that maybe Brandon was going through some changes and would come around. I quickly disagreed and told him that I didn't see a good change. I reminded my Pastor of Brandon's agreement to do whatever it took to keep our marriage together. Yet, Brandon continued to do the opposite.

The Pastor suggested that I leave Brandon alone, and allow him to come around about what he wanted to do. The Pastor also told me to keep my cool, while I wait it out and maybe Brandon would come around.

When I arrived home, I reminded Brandon that he didn't keep his promise about doing everything in his power to keep the peace of our marriage. He went on to say that I wasn't keeping mine either and that he was tired of me blaming everything on him.

Even though I knew he was just repeating my every word. I continued to say that I was tired of being the man in the marriage and he needed to step up to the plate and take on his responsibilities as a man. I waited and waited trying not to say too much to him about anything, but that was impossible when I needed his help. He did try to be on his best behavior for one moment.

I just had the feeling that he was saying this stuff to get me off his back. He told me that he was going to help me around the house more and was sorry for spending all his time with his friends.

Not two days went by and he reverted to his old ways. He couldn't help but stay late with his friends and neglect us. One night after work I realized that we had nothing to eat in the refrigerator.

I called him and asked him to bring home dinner, but we never saw it from his hands. I couldn't continue to wait for him, so I threw something together from what I found in the cabinets. I became more and more disgusted with him and his lies. I felt like I was raising another child!

August 13, 2004
6:30 P.M.

Dear Diary,

Well, I lay in my bed waiting for this hurricane named Charlie to come through our city. I went to work at eight A.M. and closed the restaurant at two P.M. due to the storm. When I arrived home Brandon and the kids were not there. Brandon got off around one P.M. and I later found out that he immediately went to his mothers with the kids. I arrived at his mother's home and we all waited for the storm. While watching the news I found out that the storm wouldn't come until around nine or ten P.M. I so desperately wanted to take a hot shower and let off some steam. So, I told Brandon I was going home; which was in walking distance from his mothers' house. I asked him to watch the kids until I came back and like always he became angry. I left anyway to avoid any arguing with him. About ten minutes later, he comes in the door and demands a reason why I didn't take the kids with me. I just looked at him crazy. Then he went on and on about how we should stay at his mother's home to wait for the storm. "Why would we continue to wait at your mom's when we were not going to stay the night? I am tired and we can be in the comfort of our own home." I stated. He then went on to say that we were living in an apartment and a house would be safer and we could come home after it passed. I didn't understand where he was coming from. The apartment was as safe as his mother's house. We didn't know how long the storm would last. I wanted my own bed and my own walls. I had a long day at work and for me having to stretch out on his mother's floor was not going to cut it. He didn't want me sleeping on his mother's furniture, so home was the better choice. He left angry again, refusing to brave out the storm. I just couldn't wrap my mind around the fact that he acted like a child. He refused to take the trash out most the time, when it was dark. Instead of cleaning, he would consider the thought, "spending time together is what we should do." I thought not. If I asked him to check the doors before bed, he would refuse and tell me to go check it instead. I just didn't know how much more of this I could take.

CHAPTER 7

MOVING OUT

The upcoming weeks were hard; the stress in the home seemed to get more and more unbearable. I tried everything in my power to get Brandon to see how unhappy I was. I wanted a divorce so badly I could taste it. I had screamed divorce repeatedly.

I guess it was like crying wolf because he paid no attention to me. I told him that I needed a man, a man that was willing to do anything for his family. I didn't want to be the breadwinner and take on all the responsibilities anymore; while he went, and played with his friends.

He told me that he didn't know how to be a man and he wanted me to show him. I told him I couldn't show him how to be a man. I could only show him the love that I had for him.

He didn't want to accept what I was saying. So, he continued to say I can teach him this manhood. I told him that he needed to surround himself around good men that knew something about raising a family. He didn't want to though; he kept giving me excuses after another saying that he didn't need another man telling him anything. Go figure.

I just couldn't help him, for he was being prideful and difficult to deal with. He didn't want to go to counseling or talk to any real man.

He didn't want me telling him what to do, yet he wanted me to teach him the ways of a man; he didn't want pretty much of anything for all I knew, except to do just what he wanted to do; which to me was nothing.

He continued to reject every piece of advice I had to offer. I cried out to him and told him how unhappy I was one night, just to see if I could reach his inner soul. I wanted him to hold me and tell me that everything would be ok and that he would truly change. He came in the room and saw that tears were coming from my eyes. "What are you crying for now?" He said angrily. His tone came to no surprise. I began to remind him of the problems that had become overwhelming.

"You shouldn't be crying, I already told you what I was going to do" he yelled! I again couldn't reach any part of his soul, if he had one.

He then walked out of the room and shut the door so he wouldn't hear me crying. I then knew that he wasn't ever going to change and I would probably always be alone in this marriage. I decided the next morning to go to work and try not to think about what happened the night before.

My mind wouldn't let me as it ran on and on about the thoughts of his ungratefulness and the hurt he continued to cause. I wanted to be happy. I just didn't think that a person could be so cold hearted. As the day went on I started to feel a sharp pain in my side as I bent down to hold my grip. I could barely stand. I told my manager that something was wrong, and I needed to go to the hospital.

He asked me if I could drive and I told him I would call my husband to see if he would drive me. I called Brandon immediately and told him that something was seriously wrong and I needed him to drive me to the hospital.

He quickly responded with anger and said, "What is wrong with you now?" I told him that I didn't know and I needed him to drive me to the hospital.

He quickly responded by saying, "Well I am working and I can't leave, see if somebody at your job can take you." I wasn't surprised by his unloving remarks. I had hoped in time of an emergency he would at least care, yet I was wrong. I told my boss that I would have to drive myself, for there wasn't anyone at the job that could drive me. I was in unbearable pain, but I had to go. I didn't want to call the paramedics since I was only five minutes away.

So, I drove about fifteen miles an hour to the hospital. I continued to think about how inconsiderate of a husband I had and how he could force me to drive to the hospital in this pain. I became very upset, realizing at that moment he really didn't love me.

I was wheeled from my car into the E.R. They immediately admitted me and told me that most likely I wasn't going home. I was scared and alone with no one to help me through the pain. I called my mother but she couldn't come to the hospital. Yet, I knew I might need her to care for the kids. The doctor came in the room and told me that he had to do a lot of tests and he would come back soon to determine the cause of my pain.

As I waited, a lot of things ran through my mind. I worried about the care of the kids. "How would I get the kids home from daycare, how would I work and how would I pay the bills?" I questioned myself. The responsibilities I handled were more of a weight on my shoulders now that I was unable to do them.

I worried that nothing would get done while stuck in the hospital. After the nurse hooked me up to an I.V. she tells me I'm dehydrated. After giving me some pain medicine the doctor came in with the news. "Mrs., I am sorry to say, but you have a very bad Kidney infection and we will have to keep you for at least three days to do some in depth antibiotics. This will prevent the removal of your kidney."

I couldn't believe what the Doctor had told me, so I question him. "Do you know the cause of this?" I asked. He went on to tell me, "The Kidney was infected through the bladder, which was caused by bacteria, which can and I believe came from a source of stress."

"Stress," I responded. "Yes, stress is a silent killer and it kills a lot of people without them even knowing it." He assured me. I couldn't believe it. All the stress with my marriage and job could have slowly killed me. I then knew I had to do something to relieve the stress from my life.

The doctor then reminded me again that I needed to stop the stress a much as possible or the infection could be fatal or cause a removal of my Kidney. My mind really was going a hundred miles an hour now. I didn't want to lose my kidney. I didn't want to die and I didn't want my children going through this with me. I had a headache not knowing what I was going to do, but I knew something had to be done.

I picked up the phone and called Brandon and told him that I had a Kidney infection and I would need him to take the kids to school for three days.

He panicked and made up every excuse in the book, as to why he couldn't take the kids to school and pick them up. My stress level rose to the ceiling, as I yelled at him over the phone. I just couldn't take him anymore, so I hung up the phone.

I couldn't believe that he would make up some excuse about his kids, when his wife was in the hospital.

I had to call my mother to get her to care for the kids while I stayed in the hospital. I wasn't going to argue with him about the kids today or tomorrow. I just wanted some type of help or support in the most needed time of my life and I couldn't even get it. I spent the next two days in the hospital alone without a visit from Brandon. I was there alone to think. I thought about everything that we had been through; including all the problems I faced alone. I wanted freedom from this hurtful world that I was living in.

I hadn't been happy in such a long time; I didn't know what happiness was anymore. My dreams were far-fetched and I was in the dark. I couldn't wait to get out of the hospital bed and return to my comfortable bed at home.

I wanted so to have some real food in my body and stop eating the horrible hospital food they had given me. I called Brandon and asked him if he would bring me some real food and the answer was the same "I am at work and I can't; you know I hate hospitals." I just couldn't win for loosing with him.

The doctor came in the room on the third day and asked me how I was feeling. I told him a lot better compared to the first day. He suggested that it would be fine if I went home but to remember what he told me about the stress.

I agreed and was relieved that I could finally go home. There was only one problem; I needed someone to drive me home. My car was parked in Valet. I called Brandon and asked him if he could get a ride to the hospital so he would be able to drive me home.

He again refused to assist me in my time of need, and made an excuse of why he couldn't do so. "Fine" I said, hanging up the phone. I don't know why I continued to ask him to do things for me.

I was wheeled down to retrieve my car in pain. "Here I go again." I thought to myself. I drove home relieved to be out of the hospital. I pulled up to the apartment and saw that Brandon was already home. "I thought he had something important to do," I thought to myself. I walked in the door and couldn't believe what I saw. Brandon was standing in the hallway, in shock that I was home so soon.

The house was a disaster. I couldn't believe it. The sink was overflowing with dishes, the garbage had created fruit flies and it looked as if there had been a party. All the food was gone and I was about to lose my mind. I dropped my little bag I was caring and I began to yell and scream at the top of my voice.

The next thing I knew, I almost reached for a plate to throw at him. Brandon was telling me to calm down. I could see the fear in his eyes, for he had never seen me in such a rage. After about five minutes of raving, I finally calmed down and told him I wanted a divorce once again.

I didn't want to live in that mess any longer. For if I hadn't snapped yet, I felt it was just around the corner. I couldn't take it any longer. I told him what the Doctor had said; forgetting that if he cared he would have been there for me. I told him I felt if I didn't get out soon, I might lose my mind. I just didn't know what else to do or say.

The more I said, the worse I would feel and the worse our relationship seemed to get. He told me that he didn't see what I was talking about and I was the difficult one. I told him that maybe I was the difficult one, but I knew how to fix it. "I wanted a divorce," I declared again.

Then he told me that he wasn't going to give me one and I couldn't make him. I knew right then and there that he was challenging me to do what I had to do to get out of this nightmare. My birthday was just a few days away and I knew time wasn't going to stop for me. We spent the next three days arguing, as cold shoulders flowed through the house. He continued to come home whenever he wanted to. Unfortunately, I had to work longer hours to make up for the shortage on my checks.

When I returned home from work, he didn't bother to wait up to see if I returned safely. Nor did he bother to sleep in our bed anymore. I felt he wanted a divorce just as much as I did.

The night of my birthday I had to work. When I got off, I just wanted to go home to ease my mind. He came home with an attitude, left my present on the dresser and left out the door. I didn't understand what the purpose of the present, if it didn't come from the heart. I knew I had to draw the line and soon.

I waited until he came back home the night of my birthday, in August of 2004 and told him that I wanted him to move out. I thought that maybe he would, since I was the one who had the lease in my name and I was the one who was paying majority of the bills. He then replied by telling me that he was not going to move out, and for me to get him out I would have to call the police. I told him that he was crazy and I was not going to turn a civilized situation into a law fight.

I told him he was evil and he didn't care if his family lived in a box while he stayed in the apartment. He then replied that he wasn't the one who wanted to move in the first place. We went back and forth about who would get the apartment. I finally gave in and told him I didn't need it. I told him I didn't want to stay another day in misery.

I could see that he didn't believe what I said and felt as if I was crying wolf again. I didn't cry wolf, nor did I waste any time moving out.

I called my sister and she allowed me to move in with her. My friends helped me move the next day. He came home from work in the mist of me moving.

He looked as if I was tarring away at his soul. I didn't want to take anything that hadn't already been torn away from me. I wanted to live in peace and happiness, and there was just no way he was willing to live that way.

I felt almost relieved that I had finally got enough guts to walk away, from the very person I felt obligated to.

At that very moment, I no longer felt I had to stay there for him. I felt I could find myself without him and I was determined to do so.

I moved that very day, without a tear or regret about it. I asked God to forgive me for leaving my husband outside the Word of God. I asked Him to heal me of all the pain I had endured over the years. I never wanted to walk away from my husband or get a divorce. I never wanted or thought that I would have to choose my health over my marriage either. I felt that if I had stayed, I would have either lost my mind or lost my life, due to the stress.

There was so much stress and mental abuse that I carried, I had to free myself of this world.

I didn't want to feel the sexual hurt or discomfort of always having infections, due to his uncleanliness or who knows, he could have been cheating for all I knew.

If you only have one partner, I really don't believe that you should keep getting yeast infections. Especially when the both of you are each other's suppose first and only. I still didn't know why, when we had sex it hurt, as if he was stabbing me with a knife.

Maybe he didn't know what he was doing, or maybe it was just my body not receiving him.

Yet, I knew something wasn't right about it.

I didn't even know if he understood how important intimacy was. I do know that true intimacy was never a part of our relationship. The love I thought we shared, had faded and I was the only one giving, while he took my last. I had run out of gas and had become empty. I was confused, frustrated and angry that my marriage had failed.

I imagined being with him forever and only being married once. I never wanted to get a divorce and put that on my marriage "record" as we would say. Marriage to me was a secret vow, that I made to God and now I was about to break that with Him.

Then, I thought to myself, "Maybe the reason our marriage failed, was, because I was a Christian and Brandon was not." I wanted to get married and he didn't feel that committing to marriage was necessary. He wanted to just live together, until who knows. I guess I would have remained the girlfriend, barefoot and pregnant, if I continued to allow him to dictate our lives. Everything that was in line with the Word of God, we did the opposite. Everything that we should have come to an agreement on, was not agreed upon at all.

I knew all the signs were there.

Yet, I ignored every one of them, thinking magically something would change. I wanted what I wanted and I didn't want anyone to tell me otherwise. So, I guess I got what was coming to me.

Yet, I felt no one really deserved to be miserable or unhappy. I truly felt like a failure. I didn't wallow in my guilt though, because I was on a mission to redeem myself and come out of the mess I put myself in.

I went ahead and moved in with my sister and her family, hoping for a change and a recovery of all the pain I carried around deep inside. I stayed to myself and prayed, asking God again if I had done the right thing by leaving.

I didn't want to continue to disappoint Him, by the wrong choices I made. I wanted to be free of the bondage and the hurt I put myself in. Yet I knew that God was the only one who could deliver me.

I continued to go back and forth to work even without an idea of how I was going to survive and start all over again. I knew that God was a way maker and he had never let me down before.

Even though I knew he wouldn't come when I wanted him to. I knew he would always find a way to get me back on my feet.

I just kept my faith and continued to work the hard nights and go to school seeking change in my life.

Brandon would call my sister's phone begging me to come back and telling me that he had changed after a week of separation. I told him no one could possibly change that quickly. I told him if he changed he would have proven that change by coming through for his children; who was two and four years old at the time. He had not once asked to speak to them, nor asked to come see them. I wanted him to change, but I knew it wouldn't happen any time soon, if at all.

After explaining to him that he failed in his attempt to convince me that he had changed, I reminded him that he had not offered me any money to help with the kids.

Three weeks had passed and still no visit. He began to quickly revert into his old self, saying that he didn't have any money because he was left with the bills. He then began to make up more excuses of why he couldn't take the time out to come see his children.

I stopped him in the middle of his excuses and told him I didn't want him to call me anymore about me coming back, because I was not and I was going to file for my divorce. I told him if he wanted to call, then he could call to speak to his children. I wanted to be left out of the equation. I didn't want to deal with the emotional rollercoaster. I needed all the time I could get to think and allow my heart to heal.

I had made up in my mind that this marriage was over and I wanted out. I quickly filed my divorce papers and made sure I did them right the first time, so the divorce wouldn't take long.

During the entire process, my heart began to feel the effects of being alone. I had not been alone in six years. Even though it felt good, my mind, body and soul still longed for "true" love, which seemed so far away from my reach. I told myself I wouldn't choose the next man that may become a part of my life, but I wanted him to be sent from God.

I knew it would be a season that I had to go through to heal. The man of my dreams was still a fantasy in my mind, which I prayed would come to reality in the future. So, to keep my mind off things, I worked. Yet, work became longer and drearier.

After being separated for about a month, I really needed a friend to talk to. There was one new employee named Craig. He seemed nice enough and friendly enough to be someone that could possibly become a friend. As I taught him the ropes of our company, he seemed to catch on very quickly. I began to dig into his personal life, as he questioned me about mine.

So, we began to talk very often and became well acquainted. I thought he was a nice family man from what he told me and his commitment to work was very apparent. He told me that he had five children all grown but one, who was two years old; which apparently was the same age as my son.

He told me he was married with a wife of twenty-six years. I thought that was so romantic to be married for such a long time.

Then he started asking me about my marriage. After hearing about his great marriage, I wasn't too thrilled about my situation. I told him that my marriage was on the rocks and talking about it made me real emotional. Just thinking about everything took me into a state of mind I really didn't want to go.

The burden of life didn't seem all so bad now. I realized I had someone I could talk to; more so someone that was willing to listen. He would stand there looking me in my eyes, as if to dig into my soul. He wanted to know why I never smiled during the day, except for when he would tell me a silly joke. I told him I really didn't have much to smile about when life was so stressful.

He began to encourage me about the good things in life that I should have been looking forward to. I told him, it just seemed out of reach to me. I forgot what it felt like to walk in my dreams and fill myself with hope.

I wanted so badly to be happy and take care of my children, but happiness felt so unreachable.

I knew that God had something in store for me; I just didn't know what or when I would get it. God had always delivered me out of the rut and the hard places in my life; I just knew that if I kept my faith in him, he would do it again.

I went to the courts and filed my divorce papers as quickly as I could. Within one week of filing my papers God already showed his mercy. I didn't have to pay a dime for my divorce, because a dime is all I had. I still felt that God showed favor in the court that day, as I handed the lady the papers and prayed at the same time. I needed God to show me if I was doing the right thing.

I didn't feel the conviction of the Lord as I would usually feel. Instead I felt a big release, as if all my pains and suffering were being stripped away from me slowly.

I wanted to feel whole again and feel like life was worth living. Nothing in my heart or body made me feel that way, other than my kids and the grace of God. I wanted to live for them and give them the world.

I had nothing else to give them other than me. I knew though that if I was unhappy, I wouldn't be able to give them truly all of me. My children knew that mommy was unhappy. I remember my four-year-old tugging on daddy and me to stop the arguing, and pay attention to him instead. When I saw my son's face that day, it was as painful as taking a knife to my own heart. I remembered what it was like growing up in a home where all you heard was arguing and fighting.

I didn't want to keep the course of argument in my home, nor did I want my children to suffer the heartache of listening to the fights.

A child can hold in their little minds the horrible events that may have taken place in their lives, but can replace them with good if there is any.

I want my children to feel the embrace of their father and remember the good days spent with him and not the sad days wasted. I wanted nothing more than to be the very best mother a child could have and protect them from as much hurt as possible.

Before I would go to sleep at night I would pray that God would forgive me, for I felt I had failed him by not listening to Him.

When I did go to sleep, God came to me in a dream and said, "BE STILL MY CHILD FOR I LOVE YOU, FOR YOU ARE MY CHILD, AND FOREVER YOU WILL BE." When I woke up the next morning I knew then that God was not angry with me. Yet I still couldn't seem to forgive myself.

I went to work day after day and little by little the good side in me began to shine.

Craig began to slowly witness to me, telling me that God of course wanted me to be happy and God would see fit that I am happy. I told him I believed it was true but happiness was a world that so many of us look for and I just wanted to be a part of it. He assured me that I was a wonderful person and many people would love to be around me in my world.

I felt flattered that he was so genuine and true to his words. Then one day I came to work and he was quiet, so I asked him what was wrong.

He assured me that it wasn't much but it was something. I didn't understand where he was leading to but I was curious to find out. After poking and picking, he finally came to me and told me that he felt as if he was falling in love with me. I was literally in shock and confused. I asked him, "How could you fall in love with me and barely know me?"

He assured me that his words were truthful and he meant every word. Now the first thing that came to my mind was his wife he told me he had. "I am not about to get involved with a married man while still going through a divorce," I thought to myself. I just knew this was not going to happen. I wasn't going to be the blame of any marriage falling apart.

I questioned him as if he was on trial about his wife and how he would allow himself to fall in love with me and hurt his wife. He went on to tell me that he was sorry. "For what" I asked.

"The one truth that I failed to mention was that, I am really not married anymore, I am divorced." He stated. I knew then that this conversation wasn't going to go well at all. "He lied to me," I thought.

I was angry undoubtedly. I couldn't believe that he lied to me when I was nothing but honest with him. I quickly said, "Divorced, how are you divorced, yet still living with your wife or no wife or whatever she is? I don't believe you; first, you told me you were married with a straight face and you expect me to believe you now?"

"I didn't know that I was going to fall for you, so I wanted to protect myself if you tried to come on to me first." He responded.

"What?"

I was so confused and upset at that moment. I knew I had to calm down to hear exactly what he was trying to say.

He went on to say, "You see working in restaurants young girls like yourself, always try to come on to the managers for a sexual lawsuit. So, when I work I tell them I am married and they seem to back off. I did lie to you but I am truly divorced and I will bring my divorce papers just to prove it."

"Ok, bring it, I want to see them." I just wanted to see if he was finally going to tell the truth.

He agreed to bring in the papers the next day and then he would explain to me why he still lived in the same house with her.

I went home that day thinking that this man had lost his mind. I couldn't help it as my mind rambled on, "Here I am going through a divorce and he tells me that he's in love with me! I just met him about six months ago and I just started talking to him. I couldn't help but notice that he was forty-seven years old and I was only twenty-three. "Oh my, that is exactly twenty-three years apart; I know he is out of his mind" I thought to myself.

I went home in thought. "What if this man has really allowed himself to feel for me?" I could only think that it had only been one month of separation and the divorce was not finalized yet. I couldn't sleep thinking about the, "what if's" and the possibilities that if this man was telling the truth about his divorce; "Then maybe just maybe he would tell the truth about the way he felt." I was just scared of what the outcome could be. "What if I allow myself to have feelings for this man and let my guard down and get hurt again?" I thought to myself.

My mind raced with fears and rivers of wonders of how this man could hurt me and if I really wanted another relationship after the divorce was final. "I wasn't thinking too much about having another relationship until this man had to open up my world of maybe's and possibilities." I fussed at him in silent. I hated to think that this may have been a good man and I was still tied up in a divorce.

Well, I knew I wasn't going to get my hopes up. I wanted to find out for sure he wasn't a repulsive liar. The last thing I needed around me was a man that lied. I needed a person I could call a friend.

I liked Craig, for he portrayed to be a nice family man, well for what I thought.

For some reason, I couldn't wait to get back to work the next morning.

It was like finding out the key answers to an investigation. My heart began to beat extremely fast. I didn't know what to expect or think when I finally got to work. I wanted to see that he was truly a good person and could be trusted.

I may not have been looking for love but I really wanted to feel true love and know what it was like to have a good man in my life, even if it was just a part of my imagination.

So, the thought of love knocking on my door was intriguing. So, when I arrived at work the next morning he greeted me with his divorce papers in hand, telling me that he had been divorced for two years. I must say that once he brought in the papers, I was relieved to see that he was finally telling the truth. I must admit though; I still questioned his intentions.

I picked and probed to see what was going on in his head, for an older man like him-self to choose me to have these feelings of love.

This was a mystery to me. I asked him at least thirty questions related to what I felt Brandon had done to me. I wanted to see where he stood. I felt words could never truly be trusted at that time. I didn't let my guard down but I kind of went along with the, "I was falling for you line," since he had brought out a good side in me. He helped me smile.

I began to see that my life could change and have a new light. He also assured me that life was not filled with horrible men, for in my mind that's all I saw.

"I want to believe him. I wouldn't mind him becoming mine in the future, but I have to play it cool and not let my guard down,"

I went home at night thinking about nothing but this man I barely knew. We were becoming closer and closer, as the days went by and I really started to see that he was a nice person. I asked myself repeatedly, "what was I doing?" I wanted answers or just someone to tell me that what I was about to do was ok.

I knew the road that I was about to embark on wasn't a good road, because I was still married, but the curiosity came out of the box. I started to let my guard down piece by piece, allowing him in my mind more and more.

As we worked together I caught myself flirting with him, and him with me. We began to play the dating game; acting as if we were already the couple of the century.

Even though we played the game as if we were dating, we knew we would be stepping into a dangerous territory, if we decided to go forward.

I believe the more I told him that the divorce wasn't final, the more he wanted me. He began to tell me that I was holding back on him and he wished that I would just trust him. I told him that I didn't see how I could not hold back from him when my heart and soul was in the balance. I didn't want to be hurt again.

Just the thought of giving my heart to another man was like; taking away God's heart He gave me and giving it away once again. I was scared, but not afraid of him. I was fighting myself at night not to care for this man as I dozed off to sleep.

I reminded myself that this was a stranger that had come in my life. I questioned myself, "why did I begin to want him a part of my world and why didn't my mind reject him repeatedly?" I never seemed to come up with the answers that made sense. My mind was telling me no and my emotions were running away, telling me something else. My body was imagining us making love, even though we hadn't even kissed.

My mind continued with this love affair. The more my mind imagined his touch, the more I desired it. I imagined the way he could caress my body with his touch.

I wanted to feel his warm touch he offered. I wanted him to caress me and make me feel like the woman, which I had never felt before. For some reason or another it seemed as if he knew how to do just that for me. I wasn't even thinking about the age difference anymore or the experience that may play a role but the kind and soft words that he would tell me.

On a regular workday, he would come to me and tell me how beautiful I was. I couldn't remember the last time I heard that said to me or if ever.

He would say that I was smart; full of energy, life, and the world around me was a joy. He would make me feel as though the beat of my heart was heard outside of my chest. He would give me great big hugs to cheer me up, when I felt down. I began to look for his smile in the morning, when I came to work and his warm embrace, before I left work. He seemed to know just the right place to hold me and make my body feel, as if it just melted in his arms.

When I left work, his fragrance would stay on my shirt, causing my mind to wonder even more about him.

I would catch myself smelling my shirt to catch a glimpse of him in my mind just before bed. I knew then that I was falling for him; but I still held back not to give it away too much. I would go to work day in and day out and he would show signs that he cared. He would ask me out to lunch just to make sure I ate a decent meal that day. It was a joy to be considered!

I held on to every moment as if time was about to stand still. To be treated like a lady was one of my wishes and prayers that I desired in a man. I wanted to feel like the woman God had made me to be. I knew that she was in there somewhere; I just didn't know where she was or where she went.

He started to bring that out in me day by day. I caught myself wearing dresses to make myself look more presentable just for him.

I felt good about myself and I didn't feel as if I was locked down or stuck in a bottle. We continued to spend more and more time together. I began to feel the tingling of my emotions at the base of my stomach that made my heart beat faster. The thoughts of him became endless. I knew there was something special about this man and I really didn't want to let him get away from me. At the same time those feelings of guilt kept coming in my mind about still being married.

What was a woman to do, let a good man go and wait for the divorce to do its own thing? I didn't know how long the divorce process would take. Who would know if he would be there when it was all said and done?

This made me feel at a lost. I told him that I was starting to care for him and I wanted to go further in the relationship but the divorce was holding me back.

He then told me that he wasn't going anywhere and he wanted to be with me regardless of the divorce or not. I knew then that he was true to his word. Then the question became, "will I wait or will I allow fear of losing a good man, push me into the very sin I dreaded?" Yet I was so amazed at how he could be so kind and loving during my emotional rollercoaster. It made me see a sensitive side of him that I really adored.

CHAPTER 8

A NEW LOVE

My co-worker and now boss Craig, became more than a good friend. He became the only one who really knew where I was coming from.

He was the one I shared the pains of the past with. I hadn't even told my mother some of the things I had told him. He was my friend, my confidant, a person I drew fond of. I soon realized I began to have even more feelings for this sensitive man. I wanted to feel the love that he said he had to offer.

Yet, I wanted to share some of these feelings of joy with my mother. Even though over the years I learned not to tell your mom everything; I believed telling her just enough would be the support you needed to balance your life.

My mother has always had her life and allowed me to live my life. She allowed me to make my mistakes on my own. We didn't always agree, but we seemed to find common ground. I decided to tell her about the feelings I was having for this man at work.

She didn't seem disappointed or shocked, but she told me to be careful, for I may just be vulnerable. I assured her I wanted to be loved too. I didn't see anything I had to lose, for I felt I had lost everything. I spent more and more time at her home to use her phone while she was at work. I had more privacy at my mother's apartment than at my sister's.

The person I came to know as Craig, my mother would soon know him as my new love.

The feelings of my doomed relationship, became all so clear. I felt something different from when I thought I was in love with my first. I never thought in a million years that I could love again. My mother assured me that I was younger the first time and I had a long time yet, to really know what love was.

She of course reminded me that she warned me about my first husband. She told me that he wasn't the one. Yes, she told me repeatedly, but then turned around and said, "If you insist on living in sin, you need to get married. You shouldn't want to burn in the pits of fire for fornication."

Now I didn't know what to think. There she was telling me that he wasn't the one and then telling me I needed to get married to keep myself out of the fire. I had mixed messages.

So, I chose what any young Christian would do, get married to stay out of hell. Now there I was having feeling of love for a man I barely even knew and I was scared; scared to tell my mom any more than I had already told her. I didn't want her to preach at me again. I couldn't help but feel the fear inside that I didn't know what I really was getting myself into. God is my witness, I prayed to him every night for direction.

"Craig wanted to love me, and he wanted to be there for me, I would be a fool to let a good man walk away," I thought to myself. I felt this was not just any person. I confided in my friends to see if I had some support.

Their advice was to stay away. They had their doubts and so did my mother. Yet I felt this was not just any person. I felt he could be my match made in heaven, but no one seemed to see what I saw. This was a man that I pictured to be a real man, my real man.

I couldn't believe that I was or had fallen for a man that was twenty-three years older than I. He was the same age as my mother. I wasn't too thrilled about that, but I quickly got over it. When it all began, this friend became so much more to me than I had ever known could be. I bitterly laughed in his face. It didn't feel real; this man wanted to have me and hold me like I was his own. He wanted me to love him the way he could love me. He wanted to be my lover, support, and friend.

I was afraid, but not so afraid. I was afraid of resentment. I was afraid that he would leave me. I was afraid that he wouldn't give me the love that I would give in return. A fear of rejection was in the back of my mind. With all those emotions running through my head, I wasn't thinking about the positive things. Even though it had been one month ago I left Brandon, it felt like a lifetime had passed and changed everything.

I talked and talked about Craig until my mother didn't want to hear about him anymore. She started saying negative things such as, "you're moving too fast and it seems as if you are putting him on a petal-stool." She seemed to act as if she liked him when she saw him but when we were alone she kept at it. "Maybe he's not the one, it sounds like he has some skeletons in his closet and he's not being very truthful to you. You are here sleeping on my couch and your sister's couch when he should be providing a home for you and your boys."

She was unbelievable; I tried not to pay her any mind. I knew love came knocking and I was willing to give this man a chance. We finally decided to take our friendship to the next level; a relationship.

September 26, 2004
Sunday Afternoon
Hurricane Jean

Dear Diary,

I can't believe I have let myself fall for this man I barely know. I just hope that I am not putting myself back into another pit again. It just doesn't seem like he would do me the same way, even though it never seems that way in the beginning. Just keep your cool girl don't fall too deep, too fast. I know if I just pace myself I will be ok and maybe I will not fall. I have always dreamed of a man to treat me like he does. He promises to treat me like a queen. I never even thought of myself in that way, but it does sound nice if he is truthful. I always wanted to feel like I was a woman and he does bring that out in me. He opens my door for me and pays for my food.

But, oh my, we have crossed over into the world of sin. I hate to say though I have never in my life felt anything like it. I never felt a sensation of no pain. It literally took over my body as if I were a virgin, all over again; as if I never did it in the first place. He was so gentle. His touch was like a soft feather over my entire body. I know I am probably going to hell for this but I hope I can ask God for forgiveness before he takes me home. I can't help but demonstrate the way he showed me that he cared more about me as a person than just my body. He has told me a lot of things and wants to care for my boys as his own. I wouldn't have guessed in a million years that I would fall in love with someone else other than Brandon. I don't even care about the age difference anymore. When I think of how this man has captured my world, I plan to be his queen and give him the love that his heart desires; for I just have a feeling deep down inside, he will make my dreams come true. I pray that in all my wrong doings, I could still come to the right way. I pray that God will see my heart and forgive me for my shortcomings.

The love that I felt for Craig was totally different from the love I felt for Brandon. When I got with Brandon we were in more lust than love and when I got over the lust I wanted the love that faded or the love he didn't know how to give.

I wanted more in my marriage with Brandon than sex, yet I received just the opposite. After so long the craving for that love intensified and the desire to feel he would take care of me and treat me like his number one never went away.

I continued to allow myself to love Brandon, thinking that I could change him with the love I had for him.

"Maybe if I showed him that my love was strong he would be this strong man that I desired." I would try to convince myself. Yet it never came. I believe he wasn't aware of how I truly felt. We didn't know how to communicate, so the intimacy was never touched on. He wanted to please only his friends and family, but me and the kids was just there. He put his job first. I started resenting him for that and tried nagging him to get him to change. I pushed him away even the more because I realized he wasn't ready for the responsibility that he chose.

I chose to end the cycle of who was right and who was wrong. I couldn't bear to live in a home where I felt less of a person.

The responsible man that I wanted was not him at all. I think back and realized why I had no regrets for leaving. I felt the life of a young man was what he truly wanted; not a young man married with children.

I believe I was just someone standing in the way of him being young again, per say. I see the difference now in a man that knows what it is like to give love and a man that may not have known how to express himself. Brandon needed to find out how to become a man. I don't fault him for not knowing but there is a time where a person should set aside his pride from his wants and truly choose to grow up.

I realize that a person chooses the path that they want to walk in. When a man doesn't have the guidance of a father it can be hard to see who they are and how to be a man. But, there are ways to find out how to endure in life and be a better person.

You must have the desire to change and become a real woman or a man. I had to realize who I was and make a change for myself to make life a happier place for me.

I think about how much love I gave and in return got nothing but rejection. I wanted to know why he rejected me. One-day, Brandon finally gave me the answer that I most desperately needed. He told me he felt secure in the love I had for him, and felt I would always be there. So, he felt there was really no reason for him to show anything.

He felt we would always be together, and I would never leave no matter how he acted. That is where he made his mistake. I felt that if I didn't love him I was doing something wrong, because I had loved him for so long.

My pattern of thinking had true enough begun to change and I stopped thinking about his well-being and started to think about mine and the kids.

I was out looking for happiness from within and to find my own happiness in living. I didn't want to go home and argue with a man about anything. I didn't want to argue about my dreams, my desires, my wants or my needs. I wanted to feel no strings attached when it came down to my future.

Craig never told me that he was the better man for me but he told me how he would treat me, if I were to give him a chance. I constantly watched this man that wanted to love me for me; for I would love him for him. I chose to keep one eye opened to protect my heart from being overwhelmed with desire.

I watched and compared him to Brandon and how the worlds were different. I watched to see if he was an ideal man, and not a pimp looking to get laid. I watched to see how he acted at work around people, compared to when we were in private.

He didn't change. He showed me that he was who he was, an honest man looking for love.

He never treated me as if I was a child or less of a woman due to our age difference. He wanted to show me that he was truly sincere and he meant what he said. In the back of my mind it was still too good to be true.

I couldn't believe that out of so many women in the world, why would this man choose me? I didn't understand that. I wanted answers from God; for he knows everything before it happens. I felt he would surely have an answer for me.

Even though my faith in God was strong, it wasn't strong enough to keep me from falling. I had let my walk for God fade but not my belief. I wanted to feel his presence in my spirit, but I felt I was the cause of him waiting close by until I got my act together. I felt that God wanted me to come back to him so he could open my eyes again. I just didn't know how to do that when the hurt of my marriage had buried my spirit so deeply.

So, because my slack had caused me to miss church, I decided to look for a church home to grow in Christ. I knew that once I got back in, I would be safe again under His arms. It seemed the more I reached out to God, the more I had to choose a road to travel. I wanted to take the road that would lead me to less pain and hardship.

The road I chose was a road to have a new love. Yet I found out it wasn't the right way to start my journey. Even though Craig had proven himself to me. It was expressed that, all he truly wanted to do was love me. Yet, I needed to return the love and my faith back to God.

"Maybe something good would come of this and I would be able to be happy in the end" I thought to myself.

October 3, 2004

This was my prayer

Dear Diary,

I prayed for love and all that it must offer. I prayed for a man to comfort me and give me what I wanted and desired.

I prayed for the dreams to come true and be so real. I prayed for a never-ending love and hope of being the woman for this man I prayed. I prayed that God would hear my need for love and fulfill that with the will; the will to have someone to touch me so gentle and so sweet; to make me feel; the will to make love to me and never have sex; the will to love me unconditionally with all my flaws; the will to keep me close and never push me away, for I am as gentle as the petals on a red rose; for this love I have prayed for, God has given to me in these endless days I prayed.

It had been one full month since our initial relationship began and things continued to move on. Craig went out of town to visit family, while I continued to work as usual. I never thought the urge to need someone as badly as I did would be a part of my desires. When I woke up that morning I was dragging and wondering why.

It really didn't hit me until the dragging continued. It was followed by a headache and nausea. I wasn't happy by this moment, telling myself it's ok and it is all in my head.

The nausea kept coming and the weird feelings in my stomach appeared to the norm. I knew sometimes my nerves could get the best of me, but now I was worried.

The thought of pregnancy flooded my mind. I didn't want to be pregnant at all; I didn't need to be pregnant. We had only done it once. I thought that getting pregnant the first time only happened in the movies.

"It was just too unreal," I thought to myself. I didn't know how he would take the news when he arrived home. "Would he be ready to deal with whatever came along? Was I even ready to deal with whatever may come?"

I didn't even have a place to stay and the last thing I needed was another life for me to care for. "Wow, the consequences of sin were large."

When he returned, the first thing I did was call him and tell him I wasn't feeling like myself and I needed to see him face to face. He was kind of baffled. I told him I might be pregnant and we needed to find out right away. He was in disbelief because it had only been once. I told him I was thinking the same thing.

It was a nightmare. "Here I am again, surly to be condemned to the pits of fire. My divorce had not yet finalized and sure enough there could be a baby. Another life inside of me that we would be responsible for. A life that we had not planned for, but would come whether we liked it or not; unless we did the unthinkable."

Yes, horrible thoughts came across our minds like a time bomb. "What to do? Are we happy or sad? Are we going to be able to support this child or will we all live on the streets begging for food?" I thought. We both had no clue. So, we took the test and the doctor verified that we were pregnant.

However, we had to make up our minds quick about what we were going to do, for the weeks seemed to pass us by, after the news and this little being inside of me was growing.

We argued, we fussed, and we even broke up for twenty-four hours. The emotions were all over the place. I panicked. I tried to figure out if this man would live up to all he had told me, for he seemed washy at this moment.

We went on and on about if we should keep the baby. Both of us didn't believe in abortion but that horrible thought in our mind tried to creep in. Time seemed to outweigh our decision. I had grown and ten weeks later the evil thought was a thing of the past.

Craig was really having a tough time dealing with it. He was happy one minute then unhappy the next minute. He decided to get another job and work to bring more money so he could move out of his ex-wife's home.

He was still living in the house with his ex-wife, paying her bills for one more year he claimed. He told me that he had been there for two years divorced and had planned to stay just for the support of their son. I was trying my best to understand about the situation but it didn't sound like it was all what it was cracked up to be.

We stopped spending as much time together since the pregnancy. No going out, no dinners, no fancy hotels, just work. I even missed a lot of school due to my two-year-old becoming sick with bronchitis. I was living from paycheck to paycheck. When a better job was offered, the hours were not available to fit my day. My car insurance, the car payment and the other little bills, that had followed me were all due and piling up.

It seemed I had dropped myself right back into another hole again, as it hit me all at once. Our relationship was a concern too. I wanted to know where our relationship was going. I hardly saw him, because he worked so much. I wanted to know where I fit.

I began to feel as though he had placed a wall up. I questioned him about his sudden change. The questions began to flood my mind, "Why can't he spend more time with me? Why do I feel as if he is keeping secrets from me?" My emotions were running wild and the need for his attention grew.

I informed him that I needed him with me so "we" could build our relationship or he could keep the life that he had in the past. I felt he was at a tug-of-war with his ex-family and the new family he claimed he wanted.

I noticed that he had changed and I was afraid of the outcome. All he did was work. I began to think he was avoiding me and the reality of the situation. The love that we shared, I still felt. Even in the mist of our confusion.

It became apparent, we wanted this child more than we knew. We wanted each other, and we wanted this family we were building. So, after all the tension left, we decided to tell my mom the unexpected, but blessing of a new baby. She immediately thought we were joking. I knew inside that she had her doubts about our future, but she held it in for the moment.

Time went on and our love for one another grew stronger than anything I had imagined.

We went through the roller coaster of feelings and misunderstandings, just trying to get to know and understand each other. Craig finally understood what my wishes were.

We planned to move in together so he could support me in my most needed time, financially and emotionally. We both didn't know how we were going to come up with the money to pay down our debts, but we still had faith in God that he would have mercy.

With the two incomes combined, we managed to receive just enough money, to move into a two-bedroom town home that my stepfather no longer could afford. When income tax rolled around, it sealed the deal. At five months pregnant, I still felt obligated to work and help pay the bills. The new job that I wanted, was still there for me so I took the position.

Craig kept working his two jobs to help balance out the income. We were content at the time and didn't worry about the bills. We knew that we couldn't control what took place in the future.

The next day my mother came by our new place to show her support; well I thought. I began to see a change in her the more. One day, I needed to go to the store for a few minutes.

Craig stayed at the house. When she arrived, she stood at the door waiting until I got back. I asked her what made her stand at the door like a lost puppy. "Oh, I didn't want you to think anything was going on," She stated. I couldn't believe she would even think such a thing.

Nevertheless, she thought I thought like her. She told me that I was the one insecure about Craig and I was like that with everyone else too. I had no idea where she was getting this from. I felt it was her insecurities coming out and she wiped them on me like a stain.

She was convinced and nothing I could say could change that.

I just knew she had lost it and our relationship was never the same after that very moment.

She began acting very strangely around me, as if I was out to get her.

My mind, body and soul were focused on my relationship and the struggles we had to face. I didn't have time to worry about what she was thinking or trying to think.

Even though the bills were getting paid and things seemed to start falling into place, my emotions would still seem to get the best of me.

Craig still would go every other weekend to take care of his son at his ex-wife's home. The thoughts flooded my mind and made my emotions take me for a ride. My heart would pound deeply, as I missed him more than words could say.

Time seemed to go by slowly and the silence in the house, seemed to make me miss him even the more. I did everything in my power not to think of him, but it didn't work.

I craved the air he breathes. The soft touch of his gentle hands; the embrace of his strong arms and the passionate love he would make to me. I craved his voice and his warmth. I needed him to be next to me so I could sleep. I would ask myself "How can a person love someone so deeply that it makes you want to cry." I wanted him all for myself. I wasn't trying to take him away from his son. I just couldn't bare him staying two nights at his ex-wife's home.

I felt she had him long enough; it was now my turn to enjoy him. I tried to fight the feelings of jealousy, but just the thought that she was taking advantage of his good will made me mad. I just knew deep down inside she didn't want to let him go completely and this was a way to keep him, even if it was just an allusion.

It just hurt a little. I imagined how he would feel, if I did what he did. If I stayed away at my ex-husbands house for two days and left him home waiting for me to return; I just knew he wouldn't have been able to take it. I felt she didn't deserve the convenience of him being at the home they once shared. I felt as if the days away were stripped from me, even though I knew he was gaining closeness with his son. I didn't know if the feelings I had were even fair, but I did know that I didn't want to continue our relationship in this manner for too long.

I wanted the answers. Whether it would be a permanent situation or would I have to try to bury the feelings that were pulling on the inside. "I really needed to catch my grip, because we did grow to have a wonderful relationship,"

I told myself. I just didn't know how I would feel, once the baby was born, if he continued to leave. I didn't want my crazy feelings getting in the way of reality or our happiness.

Even though my feelings seemed to have a mind of their own, I didn't waste any time telling Craig just how I felt. It was only fair to me and my kids to know where he stood about the situation. I spoke to him softly telling him just how I felt. I explained that there was no doubt in my mind, that he wouldn't cheat on me with his ex but the thought had slowly tried to creep in.

My main concern as I reminded him was, the time lost and the time she had taken from the both of us, that was no longer hers to take.

I assured him that he was allowing himself to be compromised by her wills and wants. She has depended upon him for all those years and because he had provided for her, she just couldn't seem to let go.

"Why couldn't he see he was still in her shadow?" I asked myself. Children or no children, we both made the decision to be together and that should have meant change.

I couldn't see our family split up because he had a child. I knew this before we were even involved. I felt there was more than one way he could be there for his son. I felt he was giving his son a false impression of; "mommy and daddy are still together," by him being there. It sent off mix feelings, not only to the child but also to me.

This needed to have a boundary. I felt he was living two lives to keep her quiet; a way to please her and then come home to make me happy at the same time.

It surprised me to find out, that my request of a time limit to the situation angered him and it was expressed in the tone of his voice.

He briefly said that things would change when we got a bigger and stable place to live. He felt I wanted him under me twenty-four seven and I was the selfish one. I knew right then that he could be a stubborn man, yet I was willing to accept it, in the hope he would compromise.

My emotions were running from end to end at this point. I didn't know where to start or where to end. We talked that day, and what I had feared came from his mouth like a flood. It was like I was ready to hear the words but never ready to accept the words.

"I'm leaving" he went on to say. "What we had was great but now let's be friends," this was supposedly the true meanings of his words. It was now March 3, 2005, as my pregnancy continued to torture me, this is what he had the nerve to come to me with! "What kind of a man would do this to a pregnant woman and expect everything to be ok?" I questioned myself.

I felt it was like a two-edged sword stabbing me from both ends. No matter how hard I would try, I just couldn't seem to get the sword out of my heart. I felt I was stabbed repeatedly by both ends of the sword and there was no help in the matter. I was alone to deal with the pain. I just didn't want to ever think I would be in fear that he would just leave me, but I was. I had waited or anticipated for the day I would be rejected and it had finally come.

"What do I do now?" I thought. I went to him and wanted an answer of why.

I wanted a good reason why he would get me pregnant, be such a good man to me and then decide out of the blue to leave me. I wanted to know why he allowed me to love him and then want to leave me.

He answered me by saying "I have lost my patience to deal with emotional problems and disputes." He felt I had brought the anger on by bringing up the situation with his son. He then says, "the problems that comes along with relationships such as: disagreement, arguments, unhappy days and the pain; I don't want to deal with it." Then he goes on to say that, he only wants me to be happy and if he stays I may not be happy and the time we spend together would be a waste.

I couldn't believe he was telling me all of this.

Considering what I had just been through with my ex and our unexpected pregnancy. I just didn't know what to think anymore.

He was telling me in one ear that he is in love with me but in the other ear; he wanted to be alone. I was hurt, confused and really praying inside, that God could help me fix whatever I did to cause this man to want to leave me. It's funny how I got myself in this mess and I wanted God to help me fix it.

There I was five months pregnant and counting. Craig had the nerve to act as if he didn't want to be with me.

It was eating at my soul. The emotions I felt were almost unbearable. I sat there alone, waiting for his return from his son's home and my heart felt as if he had ripped it out. How can someone be so good to you all of time, then throw a bomb that he's tired?

"I think he was just scared of committing again and I was the one who had to suffer." I thought. His last marriage had put a damper on the way he truly felt, but I could see the love he has in his heart for me.

He does everything for me that a woman could ever wish for and makes sure I want for nothing. The following weekend, when he returned from his son's I just couldn't help, but bring up the conversation that we had about him being tired.

God knows I didn't want to lose this man. He had been the best thing that could have happened to me now in my life. I told him I wanted to talk to him and he gave me a look, as if I was the enemy. I asked him, "What have I done to make you not want me anymore."

He tells me, "It's not you but it's me." I really didn't understand what he meant at all. I wanted to get deep down to the bottom of things, to find out the truth behind his words.

I was so hurt by the way he acted, I told myself I wasn't going to cry or let him see me cry. I didn't want him to know how weak I was for him. I went repeatedly in my mind about how and why I allowed myself to get so attached to this man, in such a short amount of time.

I quickly got off the bed, giving him my last words "you shouldn't have ever messed with me or told me you loved me, you lied to me and you should have just left me alone from the very beginning." I felt as if my feet were about to be taken right from under me. I walked into the bathroom and kept telling myself, "hold it together; everything is going to be all right, I am strong and I can make it on my own."

March 12, 2005

Dear Diary,

I woke this morning at twelve o four A.M. and I couldn't go back to sleep. This man that laid next to me sleeps as if he did nothing wrong the night before. I ponder over the situation and he has succeeded to make me cry once again. As I sit up in the bed hurt so deeply, I stare at this faceless man in the dark, I wonder if all his actions were real. Why would he want to hurt me like this and leave me in the pregnant state that I am in? Is he so stubborn that he would leave a love that is so deep? How could he do this to me, I asked myself again and again? Damn him for coming into my life and saying he's committed and then saying he's walking away because he can't have his way. How dare he come in my life and give me everything I have ever asked for in a man, love, respect, and honesty and then want to take it away. Now I question, was it all a lie? Was he a fake? How dare he walk away from this child that I carry for him and my children that have grown to love him as a father figure? God knows I didn't understand what was happening. Maybe God was trying to warn me in my dream and I just didn't see the signs. As I ponder about all the doubts I had I began to pray and cry: cry and pray. I still couldn't grasp the whole picture, because this man had been nothing but good to me and I still believed deep down in my soul that there is a good explanation for this behavior.

CHAPTER 9

LOVE HURTS

I turned on the shower and slowly stepped in. I let the water roll down my face, hiding the thought of tears.

As the water continued to run down my face, unable to hold back, the tears began to flow. I kept hearing the horrible words in my head, "I am leaving you," I knew right then I would be alone. I washed my body over and over, as if to wash away the pain that I felt. As I came to, I stepped out of the shower too overwhelmed to stay standing.

I broke down crying as I fell to my knees. The tears flowed like a river, as my body shook. I didn't realize that my cries became loud enough for Craig to here from the other room.

Before I knew it, he came in, picked me up off the floor and carried me into the bedroom. He began to yell to capture my attention, "Stop crying baby," as the tears continued to flow uncontrollably.

He said in a calm voice, "You have to stop crying or you will make yourself sick." I gathered my emotions that felt torn inside, as if he had just ripped my heart out stamping all over it.

My body still shook from crying so intensely. He grabs me to hold me telling me he never wanted to hurt me. The way he began to act came to me by surprise. I had been going around in circles about dealing with my emotions and fear of abandonment.

The fear of being left alone almost consumed me. I had no idea that Craig had issues of his own, that he was struggling to deal with. Unfortunately, I was the one to experience his wrath of how he dealt with it.

Abandonment kept rising in my mind like a flood. I had given this man my whole heart and nothing less. He has shared his love with me and had the nerve to say he wants to take it away! When I thought of my past rejections, I felt I might be abandoned again.

We talked about the situation with him keeping his son at his ex's home rarely, but agreed he would help her for one year.

Six months had already passed and I just wished that this were the end to my worries. I had to learn to deal with my problem or bury it and never bring it out again. I began to confront myself about the insecurities that I faced.

I focused on what caused me to feel lonely and unwanted. I focused on the fears of being hurt and not received by Craig. I knew that confronting these feeling head on and telling them that they no longer could control me, would free me of this headache. I began my confrontation with a prayer to God. I asked God to take away this pain that I carried so deeply. The pains kept cutting away at my heart trying to cripple me. These were pains that came from my previous marriage and were now trying to consume me.

I began to pray: *Lord I need you to take away this pain in my heart, for you are the only one who can keep me from falling. I love this man with all my heart and I know it was only you that gave him to me. Lord can you help me confront this fear that is trying to take over, for you have told me not to be afraid? Lord I no longer want these feelings that linger inside. Lord I give them to you and I release them in your name I pray, Amen.*

I prayed this prayer every chance I got to destroy the feelings that tried to arise. "I have to destroy these feelings." I kept telling myself.

Craig continued to watch his son every other weekend and when he was away, I continued to tell myself that he was a good man and I had nothing to worry about.

I fell asleep as the hours passed. I felt the sensation of his big strong and gentle hands rub my side. He had returned home without me awaking. He turns to me and says good morning, as if he was trying to apologize for the last couple of weeks. Yet, I returned the greeting.

He finally explained to me that there were women in his past that would push him repeatedly and then cry just to get their way. So, he made the threat of "I'm leaving you" to keep me in a place of submission.

What he failed to realize was, he was hurting me and causing confusion. I didn't need him to make me submit, I was already a submissive woman. We both needed to let our past go before it messed up our future. We have had this conversation before, but who would've known that we both would struggle at the same time.

He mentions to me, he had never been with a woman that was not as depended upon a man as most. He saw how I liked to get things done. He saw that when I said I was going to do something, procrastination didn't follow. I told him I always felt I had to be the man and wore the pants in the home. After that statement, he wasn't sure if I would let him be the man in our home.

I assured him I wasn't going to over step him as the man. I wore the pants six years and I wasn't trying to go back.

My insecurities began to rise as I thought about the future. I so desperately wanted to live right by God and marry Craig. I knew that my divorce had to be finalized first. Unfortunately, we had settled into this life of sin and the fears and reality of a new marriage was becoming scary for me.

Now, I had about three weeks to wait before my divorce was final. I didn't want to be that married woman again and separated in mind, if we were to marry. I wanted a marriage that would last for a lifetime. I knew that God was powerful enough to do just what I had asked for, if I asked him to.

When I finally received my divorce papers I couldn't have been more ecstatic. We had been waiting for these papers it felt for a lifetime. Yet it had only been five months. Even though I had the divorce papers, I still had that weird gut feeling, not to rush to get married. It was so weird because we were waiting for this very thing; this piece of paper to call me free, and I got cold feet. I didn't want to say the big words of, "I Do" quite yet. Even though things were going well, up and down at times, I just didn't want to rush any more.

I wanted to get to know him a lot better, before I made that commitment to him and to God once again.

So, our conversations went on about the trivial things that bothered each of us. I mentioned to him about the tone of his voice he used towards me. I told him he spoke as if I was going to disrespect him every time I opened my mouth; in return, he would try to prevent me before I did.

I did raise my voice back, feeling the need to defend myself. I saw by his expressions he didn't take it well.

I reminded him of his reaction to my tone. In his opinion, he considered me to be an overzealous woman, that liked to argue. I assured him, I wouldn't raise my voice or argue, if he respected me enough to not speak in a negative tone. It wasn't necessary for us to speak to one another, as if we were angry.

We needed to find out how to talk to one another respectfully.

After that day, I was still on the defense. I told myself, I would be a fool to let this man talk to me any kind of way, when

I knew that there was a better way of talking to people. I felt I had my share of being disrespected and it was over. I think this conversation was a stepping-stone in our relationship, because from that day forth we were very aware of how we spoke to one another.

I learned that the words that come from a person's mouth could truly hurt.

I became careful of what I spoke and practiced listening before speaking. I felt, when a man tries to keep a woman down or continues to put her in her place as he calls it, he may handicap her emotionally. Her goals, desires and ability to think on her own free will may become damaged and altered. She may place herself in a world of insecurities, fear and doubt.

A woman wants to be able to be sure of her-self and not have to question her own abilities and strengths. I told Craig, "God tests all of us to make us stronger, not to put us in a low place. God wants us in a higher place in Him. So, when we go through trials and tribulations, it can remind us who has the power."

Our battle of the sexes ended and we both apologized. I told him I forgave him and my heart was slowly healing.

I felt he was a big man to apologize, because I couldn't remember ever receiving one in my last marriage.

He went to work the next day and called me five times telling me how much he loved me. He would say he was sorry for hurting me the day before. Even though he knew I had forgiven him, he still knew the pain he had caused. The pain that I was experiencing felt like he had opened old wounds that I thought were healed and gone.

When he came home he reminded me that in a few days he still had to keep his son again and he wanted me to be aware. I sometimes wished I didn't have to be aware, because just the thought of him leaving for two days bothered me terribly.

I still had to pray to God for strength every time he would leave to go and keep his son. His ex-wife still hadn't found a day job to eliminate her working late at night.

I felt, I had to face learning how to deal with the situation. I no longer brought the subject up to Craig about the way I felt, but it still lingered in my mind every day. I felt, I needed to get it out so I wrote my thoughts and my feelings down in my journal, to ease the stress.

Days passed and my feelings about his son situation were still there but my focus had to change. I put the thoughts under my feet and got ready for my new and exciting day that had approached us. Today was March 17, 2005, the day we found out the sex of our new baby.

My Craig was so thoughtful and supportive that day.

He took off work early to make sure he was there for our child and me. When we became settled in the room we watched on the screen, as we anticipated a girl to appear in color. We saw a hand, a leg and then, oh my, it's a boy. We were shocked and amazed. A little disappointed at first, but we quickly got over the thought of a girl and welcomed our new baby boy into our lives.

We now would have three boys once the baby was born, even though the thought of having a little girl came across our minds briefly. God had a plan and we knew it was more than meant for us to have a son. Later, that evening we wanted to celebrate the news of our new son. We took our two sons to have pizza, a nice family outing.

The week past as the time seemed to pass even more quickly; the night came for Craig to keep his son. I realized that the prayer to God really worked. I hadn't mentioned to Craig about his son and he promised to not use "I will leave you" demonstrating his anger.

We had been working on our own individual problems in our own way and it brought us closer together in a way we never imagined. I saw Craig's willingness to change his ways from the past and he saw mine as well.

The closer it came for me to have our baby, the longer I felt it took. I was now 33 weeks and one day I began to have stomach aches.

Every time I ate I felt these pains, but I thought maybe it was just the food and maybe the baby disagreed. I waited three days and the pains continued off and on after eating. Craig insisted on me going to the hospital, so I went. Craig was still at work when I decided to go, and I called him from the hospital to keep him informed.

As I waited for the nurse to tell me I was fine and the baby was unhappy with the food, she told me what I didn't want to hear. She came to me and said, "You are having contractions and you are dilated 3cm, we are going to have to stop your labor." "Labor," I repeated. "Yes, you are in labor and you are not going anywhere, but in this nice room," the nurse replied.

The nurse immediately called my doctor and told the other nurses that I was in labor and it had to be stopped. She proceeded to place me on drug after drug to stop the baby from coming 7 weeks early.

At this point I was scared and sick. The drugs that they used to stop the labor had me going out of my mind. I couldn't focus and it made me feel as though I was crazy. The doctor came to my side and told me that I would have to stay in the hospital until my due date.

"I couldn't believe it, the doctor is trying to keep me hostage," I thought with all the drugs flowing through me. I immediately called Craig, yelling and drooling at the mouth telling him he needed to get to the hospital now!

I could remember him hanging up on me and me waking up to see him sitting next to me on the bed. I turned to him and said, "Why did you hang up on me?" With a slur in my speech; "I knew you had to be on something, because you don't talk to me that way."

He responded. I just laughed at him and told him about having to stay. He then talked to the nurse and asked if there were any way possible to ease the drugs and allow me to return home. The nurse told him that once the baby showed signs of stableness then I might be able to go home on bed rest.

I could only sleep, eat and use the restroom. Yet, I could go home from the hospital after a week of torture, I called it. I never felt so helpless in my life; not being able to do my ordinary duties around the house. Craig stood by my side every step of the way. He made sure that I didn't want for anything. Just three weeks prior to this whole hospital thing, I knew I was blessed. He was there for me after I burned myself on my stomach badly. I was in the kitchen cooking Craig some fish for dinner and that's when the unthinkable happened.

I have cooked fish a million times, but for some reason or another I had the fish in my hand and it slipped out dropping into the hot grease. The grease popped on me in bulk right onto my big seven-month pregnant belly. The grease was so hot it melted the silk dress I was wearing, right to my stomach.

My two sons were in the living room playing, when I screamed. I scared them so badly; I had to calm myself so they could be calm.

I immediately told my oldest son to go get daddy Craig, who had just got in the shower. Craig immediately scrambled for clothes and came running down to my assistance and carried me upstairs. I knew if I went to the hospital they would have made it more than what it was, so I trusted him to doctor on me. He ran to the store and it seemed he bought the whole shelf back. He knew exactly what to do for my burn.

I eventually went to the doctor, but he had already put his healing touches on the burn and the doctor agreed. I knew even then that he was there for me and would do anything to make sure I was taken care of.

Never once did he complain about washing the clothes, cleaning or cooking. He made sure there was nothing for me to do, even after he came home from a hard day's work.

The kids respected him and treated him as if he was their stepfather. They came to love him and call him daddy Craig. I was blessed to have this man in my life and I didn't want anything to ever come between us to make our family fade. I finally had a support system that I didn't have to beg for or worry about. He was right there letting me know that he would be there for us.

I began to labor every night when they released me from the hospital on bed rest, for four hours; then it would just stop. These contractions lasted two weeks straight with the same pattern every night. I felt as if a truck had hit me. I couldn't sleep anymore and I felt like I wasn't going to make it. During laboring, our finances were hurting.

Craig was working hard but the money wasn't there. He was bringing home just enough to get us by, but the bills were out doing him.

The lease had expired and what made it worse, the lease wasn't in our names and our credit wasn't good enough to get a new lease. We had to move and the landlord gave us two weeks to find another place. I prayed to the Lord for another miracle, for he knew we needed a place to lay our new baby's head.

We went on a desperate search for a new place to live. It took us seven days to finally find a place to move into right away.

Even though we were in the process of moving, I began to have emotions that I couldn't identify or recognize. I wasn't sure why I felt the way I was feeling, but I began to almost feel overwhelmed about myself. Being pregnant can really bring about change and upset the natural, so I wrote.

May 16, 2005
Thoughts to Craig

Dear Diary,

I had a rough night, my emotions; physical and mental state of mind has put a major effect on me. I just want to cry all the time. Emotionally my mind wants rest from all the bad nightmares that I've been having due to pregnancy. They are stupid and crazy dreams, that don't seem to have a meaning but manages to bring out feelings of fear as I sleep. My body is more tired now because of the weight of the baby. He's so heavy he's hurting my pelvic and entire body. I just want to take a walk and walk him down so he can finally come out. I want things to get back to normal, that way I can do things around the house again. I just want to scream. I just feel helpless and like a baby that needs to be held and hugged always. My hormones are off the chart and all I want to do is make love to Craig, all the time. I crave to feel his hands rubbing my aching but craving body. He has made love to me 3 times since I've been home from the hospital, being very gentle with me, knowing I am already dilated. He has stimulated me in other ways to comfort me and to give me sleep; there was a craving for him on the inside that did not want to go away. We try to please one another on a level that we both are satisfied, but the out of control cravings makes me feel unappreciative. To feel his hands gently massaging my breast and kissing my body all over to ease my mind is like no other. Am I asking for too much? I seem to want a lot now, but it doesn't stop me from giving him what he wants. If it is three times a day, he'll get it. I will scratch his back, give him a massage, rub his feet, head, butt, and whatever else he may want. I make sure his needs are met. I must satisfy my man that is working hard and pays all the bills. I just don't know about me right now. I just feel like I want to cry and flood the pillow. If I cry he may see me as a weak person. Deep down inside I know that I am a strong woman. I don't want to be looked down upon as if I can't hold my own. Sometimes I may get my words mixed up when I am trying to express myself and he may think I am unhappy. I may be a little confused at that time because I am overwhelmed with emotions all at once. My mind wants to get everything out but mixes it up instead. "So, bear with me so I don't feel alone." This is what I want to tell him all the time. I just want to be understood and not taken the wrong way. Give me time to put my words together. I want him to stay happy like he is but in a way, I am afraid to express my crazy emotions. I want to know that my desires are simple and not obsolete and not demanding. Being pregnant can alter your emotions and mind. I know I must travel this road but it is nice to know that he supports me even when I seem out of my mind. All I ask of him is to have the will to hear my cry. I want him to always lift me up and never judge me.

CHAPTER 10

EMOTIONS TO THE WIND

Craig and I had finally found a nice apartment to move into and my mother asked if she could come along because she had been evicted from her place. Well we didn't want to leave her alone, so we agreed to let her stay. Within three days after moving in I went into labor, for the last time.

We had our beautiful baby boy weighing six pounds and one ounce. I couldn't believe the instant love I felt for our new son. He came out just as beautiful and innocent as any child would. I was a proud mother of three and now the man of my dreams can share this happiness with me.

I can't believe the thought of not keeping our son even crossed our minds. That would have been the mistake of a lifetime. I would have never forgiven myself, knowing that I didn't give my child a life. God was with us every step of the way and we could bring home a healthy bundle of joy. Even though he was five weeks early God made it that he was developed completely and he was healthy.

In the mist of our happiness our finances had not gotten better and it didn't make the burdens of our heart lighter.

We were continually reminded that I was no longer working and it would be a while now that the baby was born.

Craig was still bringing home just enough to feed us and get him back and forth to work. The rent was late and short every month and we didn't know how we were going to continue like this. I prayed every night for my man. I prayed that God would give him the strength he needed to continue through the day. I knew it was frustrating knowing we were struggling to provide for the family he cared about.

We went from paycheck to paycheck and though my mother was there, she couldn't work due to an injury to her back. The bills started to pile up more and more as we focused mainly on rent. The lights were just as much as the amount of his check and food was becoming very short.

The car loan was not getting paid at all, and we were now three months behind. The car insurance had already expired and we feared the worst, losing my license. I told Craig and reminded myself, "God will take care of us and these material things were not as important as our family."

I had the faith that God would provide no matter how bad it may have looked. I could still feel Craig's emotional pain. I let him know that no matter what happened I was behind him one hundred percent. I chose to stand by his side through the good and the bad.

I started to feel, that getting to know my mate more was on the map. I was still trying to figure him out, for we had now been together for a year and I still felt the need to get inside of his head. The year was coming to an end and it seemed the more we got to know one another, the more the changes appeared. We had some good days and some bad days, but the love we shared for one another grew un-doubtfully.

On a beautiful September evening, the kids were outside riding their bikes and the sun was just setting on the horizon. The baby was inside with me. As he slept on the couch next to me, I watched through the front window.

Craig was out with a friend as I sat on the couch trying to remember the last time I had a girl's day out. I was enjoying the time spent with the kids but at the same time, I felt I needed some space for myself. "I believed it had been two years ago." I thought to myself. In fact, my birthday was the last time I went out with the girls.

"If I could get the opportunity to get out of the house, maybe I wouldn't feel so confined." I thought to myself.

Even with all the thoughts of the need to escape, my spiritual walk with God was still a high priority that I needed to take care of and soon.

I couldn't help but think about the lifestyle I was living.

The walk I was demonstrating, was not unto God. I felt my soul constantly convicted and in need to have change. I wanted to get married, but at the same time, I knew the money wasn't there, nor was I emotionally ready to take on another marriage.

I just knew that God heard my prayers and would provide for us. I knew He would soon, help us through the problems we faced in our life. I did know that God was waiting for Craig and me to come together as one, before He made his move.

I just wanted the love of God to rain in our lives together and both of us to be on one accord. I wanted us to be able to pray together and read the word of God together. By doing this, I had the faith that God would honor us for being obedient to him and not give us more than we could bear.

The troubles that we faced may seem overbearing sometimes, but I didn't look down, I kept my head up to God and continued to pray for our strength in the Lord.

I just wanted change to come so badly, I had to lock myself in my room and cry out to God in prayer.

I prayed: *Lord I'm crying out to you right now asking you to forgive us; forgive us for not living your word; forgive me for not being your child you've called me to be; Lord I know you put me through this to bring me back, and Lord I ask you once again to help me; show me the way; show me how to be a better child of God; I don't want to keep living like this; a life of struggle; a struggle for seven years has been on my shoulders and it has been*

so long in this wilderness. Lord I pray that you hear my cry and
my plea to not turn your back on me. AMEN.

I prayed this prayer with a sincere heart hoping that God still heard me. The struggle almost seemed as if it would not end. I was determined though to have a new year, a new beginning.

November 4, 2005
1:11A.M.

Dear Diary,

My mind is doing a lot of thinking right now and it's not allowing me to get any sleep. Craig is out of the house watching his son tonight. I have chosen to use this time to analyze myself to make sure that my state of mind is ok. I don't want to exaggerate on any of the emotions I may feel or think I am feeling. Our ways of communicating have changed. He talks to me as if he's a perfectionist. What I mean was; I felt he's always correcting me in everything I do or say. When I drive, he's telling me how wrong I am driving and I feel as if I am taking a driving course. When an idea has come to mind, I bring it to his attention, he tells me if I don't do it the way he has suggested then it won't work. If I disagreed with him then he would say; I was the one that thinks I know it all. He had some nerve telling me that, when I knew he has the big head. I don't like the way he has decided to express himself and I will let him know exactly how I feel about the issue. It seems he has forgotten to be considerate. I can't remember the last time he said thank you for driving all the miles I must drive, because he doesn't have his license right now. I can't remember the last time he said thank you for having the house cleaned and having dinner done before he got home. It has been a good minute and I think he has *gotten complacent in his ways. I do recall telling him how much I appreciate him and how much of a good man and father he has been. I make sure I tell him at least once a week to keep him encouraged. I let him know that I am backing him up and whatever he needs I am there for him. I can remember not so long ago we were a team and now he has seemed to forget that we must be a team for it to work. I am a person not a machine to be misused. I am not going to allow another man to control me. I don't care how much I love him, but we either work together side by side or not at all. I am a person who wants to express herself and not have that fear of control. I want to express the desires I have in life and can share them with my man and not feel that I will be shot down and placed under his feet. I refuse to lose my self-worth and who I am. I want him to see me and not through me to what he wants of me. I will express myself and he will know about it, if that's the last thing I say.*

Through the midst of our differences and struggles, I really thought about how we didn't need any more mouths to feed, so we decided to get my tubes tied. The doctor called to let me know that I was approved for the procedure. I really didn't want to put the stress on him with another child and not on me, since I would be the one to carry it.

My body had changed and I really didn't feel my body would hold another child full term. Our son came five weeks early and I wasn't ready to have a premature baby.

We barely had a place to lay our own heads and the stresses of getting pregnant again, were all so real.

Not to mention, our son together made his sixth child and his second under the age of eighteen. So, we both agreed that this was for our best interest.

If we ever wanted more children in the future we would be able to have the process reversed.

The thoughts of weighing out all options did come into play. Not being able to afford daycare, not being able to work and the setback, brought about change for the both of us.

We were not in denial that we didn't use condoms and a new baby would come all too soon after our new baby. The doctor set the appointment for surgery and we went in a few days later. Craig was right there with me, very supportive as always.

He was scared for me and had second thoughts at the last minute, asking me if we were sure we wanted to do this. I assured him that everything would be ok and we would be fine. The procedure didn't last very long and the recovery only took one day. He cared for me and made sure that I knew he was there to support me no matter what.

After the procedure was done we could enjoy one another and not have the added worries of bringing another child into the world that we couldn't care for.

Time seemed to go on and things seemed to shift. My mother to daughter living situation changed. My mother now wanted the control. If Craig and I had a disagreement, she had the perfect advice and I needed to do it the way she advised for our problem to be solved.

If I didn't agree with her, then I was not only disrespecting her, but I was trying to be grown. I felt being grown was what I was. I had been on my own for as long as I could remember. Now that she lived in my home, I wasn't grown.

I moved out of her home when I was eighteen years old. I have always helped her with anything she may have needed and I was the one she could call on if in need of any help. I started working at fourteen years old, but I think she had forgotten that my obligation to help her had changed and I no longer could provide for her and my own family.

Over time I found myself sacrificing my needs, to help her.

She began telling me what to do and how to do it. She wanted me to clean a certain way and feed my children at a certain time. When it was time for dinner she gave her advice on how to make the dinner the way she wanted it.

I went to her and tried to communicate my concerns about the way I felt she was trying to take over. She immediately took to her defense and told me I was the child and had no right to tell her anything.

I am grown I told her, "Oh you think you are grown, but you will never be grown in my eyes," she replied. I thought to myself, "I might not be grown in your eyes mom but that doesn't give you the right to disrespect me in my own home. Telling me what to do and what not to do and treating me as if I were a ten-year-old little girl." If I had said all I was thinking, I for sure might have gotten slapped down.

We continued to have this argument about me being grown in my house and she begins to get louder and louder. She begins to talk over me to drown me out with her voice, to give herself the last words. I stand there trying to collect my thoughts but I just gave up leaving her with the last word. I walked away and the house was silent.

She didn't understand my place and what I was trying to relate to her. I wanted her to respect me as a woman with a family, as well as her daughter. I didn't want her to start treating me like a child, since she gave birth to me.

I can remember I was about twelve years old when she treated me like this. I had always been responsible and she never had to tell me more than once to do something. I don't know what made her feel now was the time to start.

She went into her room and me to mine. I so wanted to just run back and hug her and tell her I was so sorry but "I was right, she will not treat me like a child. She didn't treat me this way when I was a teenager, why in the world is she treating me like this now?"

I told myself. I was hurting. I was confused. I told Craig what had happened when he got home and he tried to talk to her. He then tries to explain to her where I was coming from and she wouldn't listen to him either. She got loud and he just walked away.

Days went by without any talking and I decided to write her a letter of an apology, to maybe get understanding. She took my letter read it and it went nowhere. She didn't even say she was sorry. When I confronted her about the fact that she just blew my letter off, she got mad again.

So, I left her alone for a while thinking she would come around but she still felt strongly about us being a certain way. When it came to her it didn't apply. That just hurt me so.

I was feeling betrayed. Feeling the sense that she was just not respectful. I didn't understand my mother anymore. She was the one I used to be so close. It was slipping away from me. I think maybe not even two weeks had passed and now she was getting back with her husband John.

She had been separated from him six months and filed for a divorce. He had dropped to the lowest of lowest and now he needed her to stand by him. She comes home one day out of the blue and ask me if he could move in.

"I just don't understand," I thought to myself, as she continues to explain to me the situation about him. "Now he calls for your help. Mom, I don't think that is going to be a clever idea." I stated to her.

"Why?" As she raises her voice questioning me.

"The management has only approved me for the apartment, yet I allowed you to stay. If I let him move in and they find out, then we all will be living on the streets." I reminded her.

"Well that doesn't make any sense because we let you stay with us when you needed to. Now that you have Craig, you just don't want me to have John by my side." She replied.

"No, that has nothing to do with it."

"No one asked you anyway. You are not perfect," She added.

"Mom that is not what I mean, when I say that. What I mean is, he may keep doing the same things repeatedly and you are the one who is going to be hurt, and I don't want to witness it anymore!" I replied.

I had seen enough of that during my day growing up. Now, she was already screaming, "disrespect," and saying, "if you don't like it oh well."

Now she's yelling, "You just don't like him," as she informs me she is moving out. In her mind it's, "I didn't want her there either."

I quickly say, "Mom no one asked you to move out."

"Well you are grown, so you can live how you want to. You don't need me, nor do you have to worry about me. You have your Craig and I will have my John, my husband!" She yelled as she stormed out the door.

That was the end of a long and dreadful night. My mother packed her bags and moved out and I felt she hated me. I couldn't say anything to change her mind. She wanted her man and in her mind, I wasn't going to stop her from having him.

That was not my intention in the first place. She had been married to this man for eleven years and with him sixteen years. I knew she wasn't over him and would rather spend the rest of her life with him, instead of her being alone for one minute.

She wanted me to be happy for her because she said she was standing by her man. Well who was standing by her? I wondered as time passed us by why my mother still resented me months later.

She would call and ask how the kids were doing, then she would say something out of the blue and we would be at a disagreement. I could no longer hold a simple conversation with her. She had made up in her mind that I was the bad guy and she didn't see kindly of me. This went on and on. God knows I even prayed that he would change the way she thought about me.

I never lied to her about my feelings, nor did I want her to be alone, but I wanted her to find her happiness with the help of God. I wanted her to live her life full of dreams and hopes, knowing she didn't have to suffer just to be happy.

She later told me that there wasn't anyone else for her but her husband and he was the only man she would ever want. She said she would stick by him no matter what. "If this is the choice you have made, then I will respect your decision." I told her when she called again.

Craig knew that my mother and I relationship would never be the same after I explained my concerns. He held me up and told me I only had to pray that God would let her see where I was coming from.

I only wanted the best for my mother and nothing less. I wanted my mother and our relationship to be like it used to be. It was strong. We had a mother and daughter friendship I thought would never be broken by any means.

My mother's worries were no longer my own. Craig and I were still dealing with our struggles of coming up with rent and bill money. I tried to hold my man up as much as possible but the stress of not being able to provide for us really took a toll. He came home with mood swings and took his stress out on me. I tried to tell him how much I supported him on a day-to-day basis but that did little for the days he came home upset.

I began to have my own worries and emotions due to the emotions that were not dealt with prior to us getting together. Stress seemed to float throughout the apartment and I needed to confront them.

I had to identify the main cause of my emotional pain and frustration. I dug deep within myself and identified that fear and rejection lingered its nasty head in my mind and soul every time I felt a little rejection from Craig.

The fear of making Craig unhappy or mad constantly hunted me. The concern of him leaving and giving up came across my mind all too real. I didn't want to be alone especially when I was feeling a sense of withdrawal from Craig.

When the baby was born all his attention went on our son. I had never experienced a man giving all his attention to the child. I told him of how I felt and he shared with me about how losing his grandson had an impact on him. His grandson had died as a very small baby in his sleep. He told me about the fear he had because our son was so small. He never wanted to experience such a lost again. I was very sympathetic about his lost but I didn't know how his new actions would continue to affect me.

When we made love the baby couldn't be out of his sight. Even though our son was so small, he didn't know what was going on, yet I felt this time was supposed to be our time to bond. I felt uncomfortable with him being so over protective with him.

My time was no longer and I felt neglected. He spent so much time with our boys and me before the baby was born. At first, he didn't notice the sudden change. I started to feel as if I had failed him as a woman and wife to be. I felt because of his unhappiness it would result in further rejection.

The alone state is like no other. It was a state that I had experienced all too well before with my ex and the feelings had not gone away. When he had to keep his son at his ex's home, it took me back to another place in my mind.

The place I went in my mind was not a place I wanted to go, for it was a place of loneliness, fear and resentment. No one should have to be in this place. When he returned from the stay at his sons, he was too tired to spend any time with the family unless it was our newborn. He spent all his time sleeping until it was time for him to return to work.

I didn't know if I was starting to feel a little depression from having our son, but I do know it wasn't normal. I had to talk to myself about all the emotions I was feeling. I was up and down in the state I was in and I didn't want to go off the handle.

I came to realize deep within my-self that sometimes I would make him upset and if it was not intentional, then we could work out our differences along the way. Also, we can learn to control the emotions we feel, only if we choose to recognize what emotions we are feeling. This was a turning point of me healing emotionally.

Also, I had to learn to let myself know that the attention he gave the baby was ok. I told him my concerns and he said he was willing to work on separating my time from the baby's time. I also realized that we all make mistakes and must learn from our mistakes.

It is our job to make the changes to correct the mistakes and make sure they didn't happen again.

I put a lot of feelings I had under subjection and brought them to the front. I believed that the more I confronted these feelings and dealt with them, the more I would be able to handle them. I needed to give myself time.

While I was trying to deal with my emotions, Craig brought my emotions to the service. Then things quickly changed. We were having a perfect evening, laughing and playing around and then suddenly, he gets mad. I mean just out of the blue with no warning.

He turns to me and says, "Leave me alone I don't want to be bothered." I was now getting on his nerves and he would rather be by himself than around me.

You would think he was the one going through some type of PMS or ESS, Emotional Stress Syndrome. This is just what I called it. The way his mood changed you would believe this was a real syndrome. I can remember it was just 4 months ago and he did the same thing. Now I had mixed feelings not knowing what to say to him.

After twenty-four hours of him not speaking to me, I asked him what was wrong. He tells me that he is stressed and wishes he could give me more than what he has been giving the kids and me. I tried to talk more to him about it and he tells me he would rather not talk further.

I felt that he was not being reasonable at this moment. I wanted to talk to him to help him understand that he doesn't have to feel this way and he pushes me away.

I didn't know how to reach him at times. I felt like he was driving my nerves. He probably wanted me to be miserable along with him. For some reason, it usually would work the opposite. When I was having a good day, he was having a dreadful day or it would be a long time before we both would have a dreadful day and he then breaks. He has gone to the extreme to sleep in another room this time. No matter how I try to put it, it still hurts to be resented.

I told myself I wouldn't shed a tear. "I refuse to be locked up in these feelings of confusion. I refuse to be pulled down because he wants to be down. I will stay up; I will keep my eyes above the water I will not drown." I continued to tell myself.

So, I decided to say a quick prayer. *"Lord Help me through these testing times. I will not drown in this misery. Is this your will Lord or is this the test that Craig is doing himself?"* I prayed to the Lord for an answer. Love is a word defined in so many ways and I simply described it as a choice.

I had chosen to go through this relationship whether it was good, bad, or poor. The main strength that will carry you through the choice that you make is God. He will give you the heart to forgive and the heart to love like he would love you.

He will help you go through the lonely, unlovely, happy and the sad. You will love them when they say crazy things you don't understand and when the communication is gone. It is so important to be able to have God in your life so He may help you travel this road when no one else is there to travel it with you.

July 30, 2005
5:52 A.M.
Self-Encouragement

Dear Diary,

I said I wasn't going to cry last night but I did. I said I wasn't going to let my feelings get the best of me but I did. I just didn't want to be here. I wanted to disappear because it can hurt so badly; to feel imprisoned in your own feelings, not knowing if I am going or coming. I wanted to just sleep and have peace. I wanted to be happy and full of joy, but the tears flowed out of my eyes. He sleeps and snores as I lay on the floor freezing without his body to warm me. I just couldn't sleep next to him when he still feels the need to be alone and has failed once again to be considerate. I felt pushed away because I couldn't get near him when he refuses me near him. I don't like these feelings of love and then rejection. Why me? I keep asking myself repeatedly this same question. God has kept me this far and I will continue to pray that he will hold me up now as well. Now as the sun comes up I see myself starting a new day. I will try to leave yesterday behind me. I will pray that I will not place a wall up to protect myself from hurt but have forgiveness for him and move on.

Not even a month after my mother moved out we ran out of time to come up with the correct amount of money to pay for rent. We had to move, again. The landlord didn't want a part of the payment, but all. The total had gotten so far behind it was too much for us to even think about paying. We again were at our ends and needed a place to go. I asked my sister once again, if we could move in with her temporarily and she said "yes." I wasn't so happy to move my family of five in her three-bedroom apartment. She also had a family of five. She was kind enough to give us one of her children's rooms, as we piled in to make it work.

The money wasn't flowing fast enough and we lost our car to the repo man. We now shared her vehicle and the need for a car dreaded my mind day in and night. I became the car pool lady, driving everyone around just to make the one vehicle work.

I counted the hours I drove; which added up to be ten hours a day. I drove the kids to school, my sister to work and then my Craig to his job. I of course had to complete the same route again when it was time to pick everyone up. I was exhausted but I knew that there was no other way. Driving the miles and packing in the time finally came to an end. We finally were blessed to get a station wagon; it held up for the next two years. I was just happy to be able to have a car to take us from point A to point B. I knew that eventually God would give us the car we wanted in life when that time came. We continued to stay with my sister until times became hard for her as well.

I prayed and asked God to help us in this situation for we couldn't help ourselves. Times seemed to just get harder and harder, for the money wasn't rolling in like we wanted it to. Craig worked his long hours and still couldn't bring home enough to do much with.

We were now paying for a car in payments and not to mention that we now had to pay for car insurance. I went to my sister and told her that we no longer wanted to place our burden on her so we would let her know what the outcome of our decision would be. She understood and told me that she also had to conclude what she wanted to do about her own situation for hers was deteriorating as well.

It had been a while before we could finally make a move, but once we did make our move it would bring us to my mother. My mother hadn't spoken to me since the day she moved out of our previous apartment. I was still hurt. I just prayed that however I hurt her, she could forgive me and we could once again have the relationship we had.

Two months had passed since my mother and I spoke last. She calls my sister's home, one o'clock in the morning and she's crying.

Mom, "what is the matter?"

"I am at work and I don't have any money to get home." She responded.

"What do you mean are you stranded?"

"Well I went to work last night and John didn't come home to go with me to work. I don't have enough gas to make it home." She responded.

"Ok, mom calm down. Where are you? I will meet you and give you some money for gas to get you home, so please stop crying."

After being out of work for a year, I wasn't surprised that she had to go back to work to support her-self. I hung up the phone. I felt horrible for her. She had been out all-night working all by her-self, cleaning a building that she said was infested with huge rats. I only could imagine where John was.

I drove as fast as I could to get to where she was. I hadn't seen her in about two months and when I finally did, I didn't like what I saw. She was tired and her clothes were wet from the water she was using to finish her job.

Her hair was short and dry and she looked as if she had lost some weight from stress. I wasn't happy to see her in that state. I asked her if she was ok in her health. She assured me she was fine. We filled the truck with gas and I told her to call me later to let me know she had made it home. I was glad to see her and I hoped that it was a beginning to our relationship again. I missed her so, and I wanted her to be happy. I didn't want to hear her crying and telling me that John didn't come home the night before.

About a week passed and she called me asking me if she could use this old battery that I wasn't using. I agreed because this was another chance for me to see the woman that is so important to me. I just wanted to smell her sweet perfume and pretend that everything was back to normal. I wanted to see her smile of approval and have the assurance that I had her on my side. When she arrived, she looked a whole lot better. I didn't want to say anything to upset her, so I kept it small talk.

"How are you doing? I asked.

"I'm fine, other than the fact that your step-dad doesn't want to come home anymore and bring home the money. I'm thinking about leaving him," she said.

I couldn't believe what I was hearing. She's telling me that she wants to leave him now that he's not doing right. I was in shock that it was sooner than later but not surprised that I would see this day. I was even a little hurt because all the hurtful things she said to me two months ago. She was not like the mother I once knew.

"So, who is going to keep the house?" I asked.

They had moved into a beautiful three-bedroom home and I knew she would be the one responsible to pay the rent.

"Well, I'm going to leave him there, if he returns. He can deal with it on his own." She replied.

She then stated to me that she would find a room somewhere with someone. She tried to continue convincing me that everything would turn out fine and I needed not to worry.

Well she left that day and I just shook my head and said to myself, "If that's what she wants, then that's what she will do." I went on every day like any other day and maybe another week went by and she called.

She wanted to know if Craig and I wanted to go to dinner. I was surprised and thought, "Maybe she wants to be around me." We got together, meeting her at the restaurant. We ordered food, talked and laughed as if everything was back to normal. I was happy at that moment for I thought that we were really going to get back into the swing of things.

On the way home, we asked her if she was still moving out. "Unless I find a suitable roommate to take over John's part of the bills or the move would still be in effect." She told us. For John had never made it back to the house; unfortunately, he was arrested on a previous warrant for driving without license and was sent to prison for two years.

Then Craig said, "what if we moved in to help pay the bills, then you wouldn't have to move out at all?"

I couldn't help think to myself, "Oh my god, what in the world is this man thinking? Is he trying to put me in an early grave? Doesn't he remember what happened to me when she was living with us?" I took a deep breath and said, "So how would we split the bills?" As if I agreed with the whole idea. I knew we needed a place to live, so arguing my point wasn't really an option. As she spoke, my mind was thinking about the disaster that drove us apart in the first place. I nodded my head and agreed to move in with her anyway.

"God be with us," I prayed to myself. I asked Craig repeatedly if he was sure he wanted to do this. I knew are living situation wasn't getting any better, so I knew we needed to move.

Yet, I almost wanted to just wait it out. The move began and once settled, "temporary stay" was my everyday thought. I kept telling myself, "I can't under estimate my mother."

The first month went by and the second month went by just smoothly. When the third month rolled up, mama was ready to lay down some ground rules. I knew if I didn't follow them I would cause her to blow a gasket. First, she wanted the dishes washed at her convenience.

Repeatedly she would complain and nag about, "why haven't you done this or that? You are so dirty and nasty; you supposed to be taking care of a man and three kids, not be nasty.

You won't keep a man long being like that." She would go on and on.

I couldn't take hearing it anymore. I had to respond to her one-day when she put in her demands.

That day, her demand was another eco of her last demand, "wash clothes, clean the kitchen and take care of your man."

I said, "Mom, why do you continue to fuss at me to do these things when I do everything I need to do? I am taking care of my man and my kids."

"You are not taking care of them like you should, you suppose to do the dishes at a (certain time) and the kids supposed to eat a (certain food) and you are neglecting all of them!" She yelled.

I couldn't believe my ears; she had put me down so horribly, I couldn't even respond. I finally got a word in and said, "Mom you are treating me as if I am a child." Now why did I say that? Ticking her off was the last thing I wanted to do.

"Well you are a child and you will always be a child." She replied. I was thinking to myself "didn't we go through this already? Didn't I hear these same words?" Yes, I did hear those exact words and I felt I needed to defend myself this time. I felt she should respect me the way she wanted me to respect her.

While staring in her eyes I said, "I know you see me as a child but you should have more respect for me than what you have been showing me."

"Respect, you are disrespecting me now by saying, I am disrespecting you!" She yelled.

Now, she had yelled so much, the tears flooded my eyes and rolled down my face like a waterfall. I knew she would never hear me. She would never let me talk.

As the tears continued to flow down my face, I just wished I could disappear from her sight. "My temporary stay needed to end, and end fast," I thought to myself.

To be constantly disrespected and treated like a child was not my ideal stay.

Four months later the nagging and yelling never stopped. I talked to Craig about it and expressed my unhappiness. He suggested I ignore her words and let her do the talking, and maybe it wouldn't get to me as much. I tried my best to follow his advice.

One day she crossed the line. I was in the kitchen cooking dinner for my family. She enters the kitchen; "You should cook this for your man instead of that, because this will make a romantic dish and you should serve him like a king." She stated. Then she grabs a plate, placing food on it and served it to Craig as if he was John.

I was furious. She had no right to serve anything to my man, disrespecting me in the upmost. She acted as if she wanted him for herself. I tried not to think crazy, but crazy it was. I hated the thought. I hated the idea that she could possibly be having fantasies about my man. I didn't confront her about it because she couldn't see what I saw. If I drew it out for her, she still wouldn't have admitted it. I decided to plan for our escape.

I wanted nothing more to do with neither the house nor the idea that she wanted my man. She received a letter from John that stated that the judge was not going to reduce his sentence, so he would be gone the entire two years.

She immediately stated, "It was meant for me not to leave him, but God took him out of my life to fix him and get him back on track." Now she feels that God spared their marriage and standing by John until the end would be the right thing to do. It sounded as if she was going in circles.

I planned secretly for our escape. I now could return to work since we had our own transportation. At work, I kept my eyes open and my ears alert, waiting to hear just the right words.

I dealt with different people on a day-to-day basis and you never knew what doors could open for you.

It was another two months, before I received what would become the answer to my prayers.

I went to work and a customer mentioned that he was renting out his condo. I immediately saw freedom. I with high hopes asked to view the condo and told him I would contact him if I liked it. "Yes, this is our ticket from the horrible yelling I had to deal with." I couldn't get home quick enough to tell Craig that this could be our possible means of escape.

The money had to be budgeted and the arrangements were made to go see our new home, I claimed. When we were driving down the road I could feel my heart racing. The thought of us having our own space was warm within itself.

We drove down this long road that seemed as if it was never going to take us to our destination. Then finally there she was this beautiful place that looked like a castle. My breath was literally taken away. I couldn't wait to get through the doors of the condo. Unfortunately waiting was what we had to do.

We went home and talked it over and I assured Craig that everything would work out well if we just stuck with the budget. God had increased our income and He made things work in our favor. We made time to meet with the owner two days later. The days couldn't get there quick enough. I felt our freedom was just a breath away.

My freedom from the constant pain my mother was causing me. She made me feel breathless and I couldn't find the breath I needed to survive.

"Why did she want to continue to hurt me when I had done nothing to her? I had happiness in my life for once and I couldn't even share it with her." I fell in love with a wonderful man and I wanted her to be proud of my happiness. Instead she shuts me out as if I was forcing my way into her heart.

The love I have for my mother is hard to place in words. I wanted her to see me for me; a young adult, her daughter, the same but different. Even though I was twenty-four years old at the time, I felt our relationship should have been a little stronger.

In the meantime, we saw the two-bedroom two-bath condo and fell in love. I couldn't wait to tell my mother that we were moving out. So that same evening we told her we were moving, hoping in two weeks.

Unfortunately, the two weeks turned into one whole month. When rent came around she was ready to collect her half, which equaled six hundred dollars. We only had four hundred. She didn't like it one bit, rambling on about how I was leaving her with all the bills and how she had to pick up the slack.

"I never once asked you to put gas in the car," I reminded her. But she continued to give me a tough time about two hundred dollars.

"Mom that's not right, you also ran up the phone in my name and it is six hundred dollars, are you going to pay that?"

"Yes, I am going to pay the bill. Why do you always bring up that bill when I told you I will pay it?" She yells!

"Because you say you are going to pay it," she interrupts and says, "then I will pay it, so don't bring it up again!"

I was pleased after much argument she heard what I was saying and agreed that we didn't have to pay her the two hundred dollars. Our plan to move continued, but my mother continued to stress about the bills. The worry was not on my mind, because come to find out, my brother needed a place to stay. He agreed to move in as soon as we moved out.

A few weeks later my sister also needed a place to stay along with her four kids. I couldn't be more relieved that now my mother would have someone to help pay the bills. The long wait seemed almost endless, even though it was only one month. It seemed as if we were still spending more money than we had intended while still living there. We made sure the food was there and we continued helping when it came down to cooking. I believe mom didn't have to do much of any cooking.

When my sister and her four kids moved in, it became a very tight space; they all had to sleep in the living room until I moved out. She waited patiently to take the room I had, while my brother waited anxiously to move in. I began noticing the difference of how my mother treated my sister compared to how she had been treating me.

My mother was now playing the favoritism game. This was a dreadful game that a small child could see. "Why in the world would she want to do me like this? Did I miss something or did I hurt her so severely that she doesn't want to be my mother anymore?"

I thought about this constantly and tried not to stress about it. "Maybe this was something she would get over, and hopefully it wouldn't last too much longer." I thought to myself. Finally, the time had come for us to move on with our lives. To begin again on our own was something that seemed so far-fetched but had finally arrived. My mother came to me and said, "You know you really don't have to move out."

"I know mom, but we do." I needed to have my own space and I couldn't stop for anything.

Craig and I finally decided to get married just before we moved out. I finally had gotten over my cold feet and was ready to walk in the newness that God had for us to walk in. Also, having our own place would give us a new beginning and the freedom to do just what married couples do. I remembered how my mom loved to nag us about marriage. Her favorite words were, "you need to get married and stop shacking.

You know he might not marry you if you don't get married soon." I responded and told her that we would do it on our own time and wait until the money became available.

Why couldn't she just back off the marriage thing? I just wanted it to be when we decided, not on her terms. We didn't discuss it with her when we finally did decide to officially tie the knot. We just came home one day and told her we were getting married and invited her to come.

After all she had put us through, yet I still wanted her there. For the most part, I still wanted her to be proud of me and wish us well. I had been blessed to get the man of my dreams.

The man that could have any women in the entire world but he chose me and I chose him. He had been good to me from the very beginning. I truly believed the reason she nagged so much was because she couldn't grasp the idea that he was truly a good man for me, so she had to find something to nag about.

I wondered if she was happy I married, or happy that someone loved me enough to be the man for me. She didn't act as if she liked the whole idea after the fact. She was very good at keeping the truth hidden.

I made sure I kept any other feelings of hurt I might have had to myself. The day to move had finally arrived and if I could just leave the house peacefully, I knew we would have a good move. We couldn't place the things on the truck fast enough, making sure we took everything in one trip. My new husband and I didn't want to come back for any missing items. Giving her the opportunity to get upset would make the whole move horrible.

I was going through an emotional search inside when we did finally move out and settle in. I finally saw just how distant my mother and I had really become.

It was real but unreal to me that she really had let me go. She let me out of her home without a fight but now I saw, she had let me go inside. Now I was confused about this cutoff that was real and not a dream. She did come around every now and then acting as if we were back to normal but I soon realized that all of that was just a cover-up.

August, September, October and November had come and gone. Craig and I were nice and comfortable in our new condo sitting in the living room watching television and the phone rings.

"Hello," I answered.

"Hello, how are you?" She asked. She used a tone as if she was excited to hear my voice.

"Fine," I answered.

"So, what has been going on mom?"

"We are moving and I left the lights in your name to transfer the lights to the new house." She responded.

"Mom, can you ask my brother or sister to put the lights in their name now; I am trying to fix my credit?" I asked her.

Oh, why did I even go there? It sounded as if she had so much anger built up inside for me, the excitement left in a hurry. She could have reached through the phone and choked me if she wanted to.

"You are not perfect." She yelled.

In so many words she said, "Well if you want the lights off and out of your name, then just cut them off on us and leave us in the dark."

The phone clicked, as she hung up on me. I couldn't believe after time had passed, she would still go off like she did. She had the lights in my name for two years and her name still wasn't good enough to put the lights in her own.

When she told, me she was still using my name, I really became impatient. I wanted my name off the lights and fast. Yet I couldn't just leave her, my sister and brother in the dark, could I?

I was lost of words, but I felt like the bad guy because now I knew she was talking badly about me to my other siblings and there was nothing I could say or do about it.

I just wanted my name back, so I could deal with the problems I had with my own past. I thought after that day I wouldn't hear from her in a while. It took her about a week to call me again and she pretended she had said nothing to me previously.

When she saw that I wasn't going to turn off the lights or bring the conversation back up, she was back to her calm self again. December came and I still felt in my heart that my mother had abandoned me for she would still say mean things to me or just things that would make me wonder about her love for me.

Ring, Ring, she calls and the conversation seemed to be decent, then she asked advice on how she could get internet. I gave her some advice and told her that she could get it through the cable company. I just knew there had to be a catch to this because this wasn't her first time having Internet. She finally tells me, "it's in your name and you will have to do it for me." I was in shock again, and very much upset. She put the cable in my name and didn't ask me and now she wanted Internet too.

"Mom, how could you, I didn't want anything else in my name," I explained to her.

"Oh, there you go fussing at me like I don't know how to pay my bills. You treat me like you are perfect and you are the only one who knows how to pay bills!" She yelled.

"No mom, that is not it at all. I told you that I wanted my name cleared."

She continued to interrupt fussing and yelling and I would just say, "Ok, just forget it mom. I will talk to you later; good by mom, I'm hanging up now." That was the end of that conversation, but the damage was done. I knew that our relationship was on the edge, like it has been for almost a year now and I needed God to help me get through to her. "I give up," I told myself. I was at a loss for words about the whole situation. I just didn't know how to reach her.

CHAPTER 11

THE AFTER EFFECT OF MARRIAGE

The more it seemed I wanted to reach my mother, the less I could connect with her.

Our relationship seemed to spiral to a no conversation basis. I couldn't seem to have a regular conversation with her without one of us getting offended or upset. I just didn't understand the tension between us. I didn't want her to feel I was against her in any way. I didn't want her to feel that I was better than her. I was tired of fighting society about credit.

When you're not able to get approved for things because poor credit is on the top of the report, it should make you think twice about your future. I hated that our struggle was preventing us from paying on our debt. I wanted to have a clean credit report, with no debt.

We live in a society that expects you to have no money, no credit and live above or below your means, keeping you in a world of debt, while they get rich. I am just tired of struggle. I want to change the stereotype that has been created.

I wanted my mother to know I saw the struggles we faced but we don't have to stay in that place. We can change what we have the power to change but it sometimes takes a whole family to help one, to achieve change. I wanted her to see that debt is not the way of life, but living without it or reaching to live better is what makes life worthwhile.

Even though I had all those thoughts, my desire to express them wasn't enough. I was unable to tell her that we could hold one another down with the simple things, when we should hold one another up.

Months went by and I didn't stop praying for my mother and for our relationship to return to its original state. She finally came around and expressed her interest as to what I had to say. We sat on my couch and I slowly spoke to her telling her all that concerned me. I cried and expressed my deepest emotions and she too shared some of hers. I concluded that her own insecurities had been holding her back from the beginning of our problems. She failed to realize that she never faced her insecurities and stated that God had delivered her in the past of all she may have had.

Yet she failed to realize that some of her insecurities and past hurts remained. We lost something so valuable over the years, which I hoped could be restored.

She said everything was squashed but from time-to-time I still saw that she continued to remain distant, refusing to get too close.

My mother assured me that her love for me hadn't changed and she would always be there for me if I needed her. I no longer pushed the subject of what happened in the past or what our relationship would become. I just enjoy the moments we did have and I cherished the kind words we did share. I never forgot I only have one mother and the love I have for her will forever grow.

May 1, 2006

Dear Diary,

I have prayed about my mother and our relationship and now I have given it to God. I have found peace in my heart now knowing that God will change what needs to be changed. I have done my part and given my thoughts. There is nothing more I can do, but love genuinely. I have been through more in my life than this and I will not let a slight difference break me. I wake in the morning and thank God for a new day and thank God for allowing me to have the priceless things in life; family. This door is now closed and I will move on with the rest of my life, marriage and family; praying that God will take me far in whatever he desires for me.

Life seemed to continue its course. Craig and I wanted to see if marriage would change one of us. It had now been one month in our marriage and it really didn't seem as though either one of us would change. Craig supported us until the baby turned eight months.

Now that the two of us could work, we really wanted to see the change in our lives. The baby was now approaching a year old and time wasn't slowing down for anyone. I did know that things would happen in our marriage, for I knew marriage wouldn't make us perfect.

It seemed liked the more I prayed the more God tugged at my heart. I finally made it my responsibility to go to church after months of not being faithful enough, to just go. I wanted Crag to be a part of this wonderful connection with God that he once had so long ago.

He confided in me telling me that he wanted to get back in the church on his own and when he did I would know. I felt that he was holding back on God, for we both knew we had the gift of song given by God, we just needed to use it for the Glory of God.

A few months passed and it seemed the power of prayer worked and he began seeing the need to have God in our marriage more, as well as our individual lives.

He began listening to me more when I spoke about his negative attitude he showed.

I communicated to him very often, remembering to keep a calm voice in mind. I wanted him to be aware of my feelings. I felt that if we could speak on a level of softness and was slow to anger, then we would have an ear to a better understanding of one another.

His love for me was big. I could really see his love demonstrated because his actions spoke louder than words. He was slowly growing and learning how to express himself with words.

He practiced daily to use a soft tone of voice. Now that we were married, we both were willing to change to better the relationship.

When he began to show me that he was versatile, I was more than pleased with him. I saw that I could express my faults, as he expressed his. To express yourself and tell someone the needs and desires you have, are very important in a relationship or marriage. I knew that I had a good man with a good heart.

We both found out, it was easier to compromise then to argue. We both had baggage in the beginning of our relationship. We both had to learn to let go of what could hold us back from being the true soul mate that God had established for us to be. It was hard and bumpy.

Even though we started out the wrong way, we began to go in the right direction. I had my doubts, even the week before we got married. I wanted to make sure Craig wanted this commitment and wouldn't change his mind once we were married. I wanted that assurance he would commit to me and be there for the rest of our lives. Unfortunately, there were no guarantees.

I had to believe that God was the only one that could keep us and sustain our marriage. He was the one who honors marriage. So, I kept my head up to the heavens and kept my knees bent in prayer for a covering. Being married to Craig really didn't change my outlook of things and how I treated him. I treated him the same and I didn't expect any more from him than he was already giving. I wanted him to just continue to love me unconditionally and I the same to him.

I started to go to church as much as I could and asked Craig to come whenever he wasn't working. He began to slowly come to church with me and I couldn't be happier. I felt that uniting in the Word as one, would keep us stronger in our marriage.

One Sunday the Pastor gave and altar call and Craig rededicated his life back to the Lord, to start fresh and new. I knew right then that he wanted God for himself and nothing I said had to be of any pressure. When the Pastor handed him the microphone, he expressed how grateful he was to have a wife such as myself that was willing to stand by his side.

I was so overjoyed that my husband would say something so sincere in public and mean it. Yet when I thought things were finally going smooth, the devil had to stick his ugly head up.

We got along fine, with no arguing what so ever but Craig had another one of his weird days. We all were watching a movie and he simply didn't want to be bothered any more for no apparent reason, to my knowledge.

He left the room and went in the living room with his blankets, as if I had told him to sleep on the couch. To make things worst he makes this statement to push me away.

"I'm taking my son and I'm leaving you because you have too much on your plate."

I thought to myself, "what in the world is this man talking about now?"

"Here we go again."

I was shocked, hurt and confused. I didn't want our relationship to start changing for the worst now that we were married. I didn't want to lose the communication that we shared so openly. What could I say? What could I do to make it better?

"Should I say anything at all? Or should I try to reconcile for something that I didn't do?" These were the thoughts that flooded my mind. I was lost for words, as I tried so hard to hold back the tears of my emotions, and not let them get the best of me.

The fears kept popping up in my head, "Simple things could destroy this marriage." I allowed my mind to talk to myself about me and I prayed that God would put the words in my mouth before I spoke. "I will not have another failed marriage," came to my mind as I sat there thinking. I couldn't sleep without knowing I had closeness with my mate. My mind continued, "My love, the one I gave my vows to, the one who I want to spend the rest of my life with no matter what. I will not let the devil defeat me; I will not let this little confusion or whatever it may be control my marriage.

God ordained this. This is a blessed marriage and it will stay blessed no matter what the hardship may be." I sat there speaking these words out of the bottom of my heart and screaming these words from the depth of my soul. I needed to let myself know that there was a greater power than this issue that Craig continued to have ever so often.

I didn't want to feel the fears of defeat, the fears of abandonment, the fears of losing someone so dear to me, even in the same home. I didn't want to relive the past again. I knew I didn't have the power to control my future, but what scared me was I didn't know if he had changed his mind about our marriage.

I could only hope that he would choose to go all the way. I could only pray, for sleep wasn't on my side. I was wrecking my brain trying to figure out what I did wrong, while he stayed in the other room snoring like nothing was wrong at all.

I wondered if he was testing me again to see how I would react to his sudden change. "Maybe he was playing a, "mind game." I just didn't know. At times like this, I wished I could read minds. I wanted to find out exactly what he was thinking and the moral behind it.

The next day was Memorials Day and neither of us had to work. We both would have had the opportunity to spend time together but now this. He didn't say a word to me and I was afraid to confront him about the whole odd situation.

He even asked me the day before to rent movies, for what? I guess he wanted the boys and me to watch the movie without him. I wanted to have a good weekend together as a family. When he had his mood swings it dampers the entire day. I felt something was seriously wrong with him.

For a person to randomly do things like this, it had to be mental, right? We are all family and if he didn't want to be bothered, he could have just told me instead of allowing his weird thoughts to control his ways and days.

May 30, 2006
1:52 P.M.

Dear Diary,

Well it took two days to find out what the problem was regarding the sudden change in his attitude. He tells me that he feels as if my future goals will be a little much for me to handle. I have so much that I want to do, such as writing books, going to school and opening small businesses. So, he felt the need to separate himself to give me the impression he was going to walk away from the family. He wasn't helping me; instead it does the opposite; it breaks my heart. It's bad when a man knows your weak spots because he can use them against you or in his mind may try to bring you back from your world of independency or whatever your case may be. For me it's to his advantage by telling me that he is going to take his son, and "leave me" because he feels the load will be unbearable. Maybe he thought it would be easier to tell me he's leaving, to convince me I wouldn't struggle. He came up with this idea that if there were less people to take care of, then it would be better for me. Maybe he was thinking that if he gave me this outrageous story and not talk to me for a couple of days I would believe it or maybe he wanted to hurt me to keep me in line. I don't know what he was thinking but I do know he must have been out of his head. I know one thing that his way of doing things will not help me in my healing process nor does it help our relationship.

We had a beautiful relationship until exactly six months later. I then found myself asking, "What did I do wrong to make this man so upset? Why isn't he talking to me?" As the blood rushed to my brain and my heart, I began to feel hurt and alone.

He would again choose not to talk to me; I recalled, for no reason what so ever. Then two days, if not three, he's playing this game of, "I am mad so let me upset her." I didn't believe that was his true intent though, but maybe he was trying to make a point.

To me he's always in protective mode. He has told me that if he begins to feel I am doing too much, then he "just know" I will become so overwhelmed I won't have any time for the family. So, he threatens to leave and take our son with him to "lighten up" the load. Twisted, right?

Well after waiting another day, I wanted to find out the real deal behind his motives. He told me he didn't know. So, I just reminded him that he did this every six months, like he wants to see me cry or upset. Then he said the dumbest thing I had ever heard. "I feel that since we don't argue we should have some disagreements every now and then to make our relationship stronger."

I felt he was truly confused about how a relationship must flow. I wasn't an expert, but I did know eventually the disagreements would naturally come. So, by him creating the disagreements, it did nothing but push the relationship in a negative direction.

Over the years, we had learned how to talk to one another instead of yelling. Yet sometimes our signals are crossed. Even though we have these different signals of how we deal with things, life, and love. I pray that we continue to grow as good friends and our love we share for one another will continue to mature. What I have always dreamed of in a man, God has blessed me to have it in Craig. He just has rough edges like everyone has, and I know soon he will be smooth as silk.

When we do have disagreements, I try not to leave them on the burner to fry. I love my husband and I know he means well, so I knew something would give. We all do and say things that we don't mean, while really meaning something else. I came to realize he wanted nothing but happiness. He confided in me one day, telling me that he would work on this problem and his insecurities.

While Craig worked on his problem, I analyzed myself. To avoid the constant hurt, a withdrawal would be the safety net I usually would take. I didn't want to start resenting him to protect myself from hurt. I didn't want the petty things to separate us. For I knew they could be handled a unique way.

I would force my tears not to flow. My mind would speak to me telling me, "be strong and don't cry." If I allowed the tears to flow, my body would begin to shake and my head would begin to pound with a headache. My nose would become blocked making it hard to breath. My body and mind just wouldn't allow it. My body knew then that stress wasn't for me but joy, peace and happiness is what I needed.

I couldn't really depict when another disagreement or separation would come my way. I knew that Craig had a problem and I didn't know how to help him. I did know he was a good man. All the heartache and tearful nights didn't add up to how wonderful he treated the kids and me. His love truly was expressed every day. I couldn't just turn my back on him because of his insecurities; for I prayed one day that he would be healed of all his past.

Life continued as usual. It seemed every time we got close to getting it together financially, a wrench was thrown in the mix.

Our 4-C finally expired and a break was not in the picture. So, to make matters worse, I had to quit my job because daycare wanted to charge more than I brought home a month.

I felt that the least I could do was make myself productive and enroll back in college. I had desired for so long to just finish school and accomplish the goals I had set out for myself. I knew that letting Craig know that I wasn't just sitting on my butt waiting on him to bring me his checks would lift his head slightly. He would always say to me "I just want you to be happy." I knew that allowing him to see me in my state of calmness would give him some type of peace. I never tried to place more pressure on him then he already had on himself. He was doing the best he could at the given time. There was no need to demand for more.

I assured him that going back to school would not only give me a piece of mind but it would allow us to look towards a future of stability. I desired a foundation for our family, an income that was stable and consistent. I longed to know that my job or his job would be there no matter what. I longed to get out of debt and the need to live from payday loans to more payday loans would finally come to an end.

Going through the motions and living from paycheck to paycheck, time seemed to fly by. Craig continued to support the family with his one check and pay his child support. I watched him every day as he came home from work extremely tired. It was like his entire world had come crashing down on him and he had to get up the next day and repeat the process all over again. I noticed he became angry and stressed when payday arrived.

The check was so small it looked as if he only worked a couple of days for an extended two-week period. He would come home with his head hanging down as if he just lost his best friend. He just handed me the check in hopes that I wouldn't disapprove of him. I could never disapprove of him, when I knew he gave his all to support a family of four including him-self.

The more we played catch up with our bills the worst off it seemed we became. The money was just not there and the rent was behind by two months. Having to quit my job really put us in a hole. The bills were coming in faster than the money. Yet I continued to put my trust in God, for he knew the outcome before the end. I continued to pray that God would hold us up through the test and that we would come out on top. I encouraged my husband telling him that God had something in store for us; I knew we just had to be faithful enough to receive it.

After we talked, Craig seemed to have more peace in his spirit. You would be amazed how your spirit can feed off the troubles that you face and go through on a day-to-day basis. I continued to lift my spirit up by listening to the positive thoughts of the Holy Spirit.

They sounded like, "*We have to be careful to be rooted and grounded in the Word of God and prayer. When trials come our way, we will not be surprised but we would be ready. We should be ready always for the darts of the devil but we fail sometimes to see when the darts are thrown. We are not perfect, so sometimes we also refuse to get back up when we have fallen.*"

I know I am not perfect when it comes down to the Word of God but I have realized that God's Word is true. Sometimes we just need to take the time to be quite and listen and the voice of God can be heard.

God gives us directions of what we need to do for Him. We must make sure, we are extending our ear to listen to God. God may talk to us directly or through our dreams, our Pastor, our children or even a stranger. God can give you the wisdom and knowledge that you are looking for.

God has given us the power to change our own circumstances by living by faith and walking in it. "If we don't believe that we can do exactly what He says He can do, then why do we say we serve Him? Who do we believe then?" So, as these thoughts continued to go through my mind, I continued to keep the faith in God and continued to keep my head up. My husband came home one day and asked me, "Have you heard about the hiring the government is doing?" I told him no, but I would check it out. I didn't' know that God was using my husband as a messenger.

Yet, I went on-line immediately to check out the job and the requirements. I talked to him regarding the requirements and let him know that they required very demanding physical and mental capabilities to be considered for a permanent hire.

The job I spoke of was in hopes to work for the government. I finally applied for the job in August of "07" and didn't receive a response until two months later. It's amazing how God test your patients, because the week before I heard from the job, I applied to the same agency in a different county. I was simply becoming impatient; forgetting that all things come in Gods timing not my own.

The day I almost missed my blessing, I called the agency in the other county to see what I needed to do to be considered for the job.

The agency told me I would need to come in and pick up the paper work if I wanted to be considered. I wanted to be considered for any job that would pay the bills. It was a rainy day and I barely had enough gas in my car to get to the gas station. I knew I didn't have enough gas to drive thirty minutes away. I told myself, "I can do it if I scrapped enough change off the bottom of my purse."

I then hesitated as I went to grab for my purse when I heard the Lord say, "CHECK THE MAIL FIRST." So instead of looking for change, I grabbed my keys and went straight to the mailbox. When I opened the box, I grabbed a letter that read, "Government Department" from my own county!

I was immediately overjoyed. First, I listened to the voice of the Lord; secondly, I was rewarded with the letter to start the process of hiring. Right there I knew that all the prayers I prayed had not been in vain.

A week later God had another test for me, a test of faith. Craig came home on payday with his head hanging as if touching the ground.

For some apparent reason, I already knew in my spirit what he was about to say before he even said it. He gave me his check and said, "Baby the IRS has taken eighty percent of my check and this is what we have left." It was a check for three hundred and twenty dollars. This would make any man not want to come home and face his family. This wasn't enough to pay more than two bills. I told my husband it would be ok because God had already prepared me for the news. He nodded his head yet his facial expressions resembled failure.

I told him that no matter what happened next, God would bring us through.

It took another two weeks before I could take the first test. Yet around the same time the landlord gave us two weeks to come up with the rent or move. Craig's checks were just not enough to cover the rent any longer. A blessing and then a test, that's how it seemed to flow. I immediately remembered mom stating, "If you need me I'll be there."

So, with all hopes of a good outcome, I did what I had to do. We didn't see any other way other than to call my mother and ask to move in for a while. Our goal was just to save and move right out. After the call was made, my mother was willing to let us move in, once again.

After the uncomfortable move, back into my mother's home, I could continue the hiring process for the upcoming academy. I couldn't wait to just be hired and move out of my mother's home and once again feel free in my own skin.

I believe a year had past and my mother, brother and sister had moved in a five-bedroom home to give them more space, now my family and I joined the crew.

Things didn't seem to lighten the load once I moved in. Two months in and my mother began to have financial problems of her own and our plan to save went out the window.

Craig suggested that we call our past landlord. Craig was curious to see if he would be willing to rent out any other homes to us, since we now had the funds to rent again. We were good tenants and when we moved he held no grudge.

Our landlord informed us that he didn't have any new vacant units but the one we moved from was still available. Moving back was a great idea, since the job was going very well.

He told us if we wanted to move back in we were more than welcome and we could start fresh. When we moved, we were not aware, financial problems would raise its ugly head into the life of the landlord.

We couldn't believe that we were able to move back into the condo without having to pay our past debt or a new deposit. So, without a second thought we moved back to the place we called home for the last two years. We moved this time with the mindset that this Condo was also a temporary setting place for us. We wanted more for the kids such as a back yard with a fence and more space. In about three weeks we were back into our condo in hopes that things would go our way for a while.

I had been working twelve hours a night for about a good month and a half, as Craig worked days, avoiding daycare all together.

The academy was about to start in a few weeks and my schedule would change from nights to strenuous ten-hour days, for four days a week for three months.

Craig and I continued to pull our first split schedules until one day he woke up and told me he wasn't feeling well. I suggested that maybe he should stay home and get some rest but he insisted on going to work. Two hours later Crag calls me telling me his face was burned from his neck up, from a gas fireball that came out of the oven at work. I couldn't believe what

I was hearing and to make matters worse, he refused to go to the hospital by paramedic. I was thirty minutes away and my heart went into rescue mode.

I told him to place something cold on his face and just like anyone who loves their husband or mate, would run to their rescue as fast as they could. I remember jumping out of bed, with the baby in one arm and then grabbing the keys with the other hand. I jumped in my car as fast as I could.

As I headed down the road, I realized I had to have been going over the speed limit because I got to his job in half the time it would have taken me to get there.

When I arrived, he was standing at the curb with wet towels to his face, shaking uncontrollably. My heart dropped in my chest when I saw that his deep brown face was no longer brown but chard. His lips were chard, his eyebrows were half gone and his jaw was chard black. While in the car he told, me he felt as if his face was on fire.

I rubbed his leg and told him not to worry, for I would take him straight to the hospital. His body continued to shake uncontrollably and he began to moan and groan in pain. I immediately drove onto the 408, and I can't lie the more pain he demonstrated, the faster I went. I told him repeatedly, "we are almost there and you will be ok baby."

I felt useless, as there was nothing I could do to ease his terrible pain. When we arrived at the ER, I ran straight in and grabbed for a wheel chair. He slowly got into the wheel chair. I held the wheel chair with one hand and the baby on my hip, pushing him as fast as the strength in my hand would allow.

Once to the front desk the nurse at the desk saw his emergency and immediately began to take his information. He was then wheeled to the back to an empty room to wait to see the doctor, as I followed anxiously.

Time seemed to go by extremely slow as I cared for him while we waited. Two hours had passed before a nurse came to check his status. I became frustrated and angry as the pain he demonstrated did not subside.

The nurse arrived again telling us that the doctor would be in shortly. Again, we waited another two hours just so the doctor could tell us that he could use a burn cream, some over the counter eye drops and make a follow up appointment with our primary doctor. I was furious, for I could have taken him straight home instead of wasting our time. "I just know they charged us an obscene amount for the cream and the drops." I thought to myself.

I took Craig home to care for him the best way I knew how. Now we had another problem.

He was unable to work and I knew right then the ball had shifted to my court. I knew that this was yet another test God wanted to see if we would pass. I had faith that God would bless to make this job my permanent job, if and only if I kept the faith.

God talks to me a lot and He spoke to my heart why my husband was suffering. I went to Craig and told him, "God wants your full heart." Craig had rededicated his life back to God but wasn't allowing God to reign in his heart completely.

Craig was holding back for some reason, not giving God his all and all. God wanted more out of the both us. Craig just nodded his head as if he already knew what God desired. We were just having a conversation a few months ago about our relationship with God.

I don't know what it is about how we follow Jesus, but I do know that most of us are aware of him. Some of us may know what our calling may be, but some of us may not. So, we continue to give or use excuses.

God is not listening to our excuses of; I don't have time, I'm not ready, I want to get myself together first, I want to do more but I am fighting my flesh, or I am just waiting for my conformation from God. God is not listening to all of that. He is just waiting for us to say yes.

He just wants us to get up off our butts and work for Him. Even I have had some excuses, whether it was waiting on Craig's approval or just being lazy. In the mist of me trying to get my walk straight with God, I still desired for Craig to be happy with me no matter what. I wanted to serve God with all my heart but still was afraid of rejection. I still feared that if I served God with all my heart and soul Craig would reject me because I was what we call, "deep" when it came down to the Word of God. I didn't want our marriage to turn into a, "Choice" situation.

I didn't want to feel that Craig would want me to choose him over God, or even put me in that place. I know my ex-husband did and I made the wrong choice, I chose him. I was not about to do that again.

So, as I continued to care for my husband and prayed that God would heal him to the point of no future complications; I worked and worked on making sure that the stresses I may have had were put on the back burner. I wanted my mind to be clear to focus on the needs at hand. As time moved along, two months had passed and Craig made a quick recovery. His face no longer pealed pink and it looked as if he had never been burned. I paid all the bills, for as it turned out Craig's asthma that bothered him on occasions flared to the point where working in a heated condition like a restaurant setting would make it worse.

Unfortunately living from paycheck to paycheck didn't go away for it just shifted from one hand to the other. I continued through it all to have faith that God had a plan for us. Even though my faith was strong the devil was angry and was trying to interfere with my faith.

My landlord came over a couple of weeks later and informed us that the condo was going into foreclosure and he was unable to save it. I knew at that very moment that God was still in the working it out business. I wasn't even angry or worried, for I knew this was a way for my husband and me to find a house with a back yard for the kids. So, we began our search, always keeping a prayer on our lips for favor. Credit was our main concern. Finally, about three weeks later we found a home that fit what we desired.

We called the owner and decided to meet and talk about qualifications. Lord and behold he wasn't looking for credit, but just wanted a nice family to move into the home. God had opened the door for us to find a place with little effort. We stayed in the condo for one more month before we made our move.

During the last month, I continued with the on the job testing, while Craig supported me from home encouraging my spirit. He made sure I didn't lack for anything as he switched places with me maintaining the home. He continued to care for the children, clean the house and make sure we all had three hot meals a day. When I came home from my long strenuous days I could barely move my limbs, for the testing was draining physically and mentally.

My body ached from my head to my toes. I sometimes felt as if I wouldn't make it another day. Craig continued to be in my corner encouraging me along the way, telling me he was very proud of me no matter what the outcome would be.

When it came close to the end, it meant pass or fail, job or no job. You had to pass a certification test to keep the job. The pressure and the stress of keeping the job finally hit home. I had one more major test and when I took it I prayed to God to allow me to pass.

The results were in and I had a slight feeling that this may have not been my day. I looked on line for my test results and Lord and behold, I saw "FAILED" in big red bold letters. I just stared at the computer in disbelief. I still couldn't believe it. With the pre-emotions that had come upon me, the outcome made me feel like a failure. I felt as if I had let my whole family down and now my husband and three children would suffer because of my failure.

I walked away from the computer and informed my husband. As he tried to comfort me, I found myself not wanting to receive his words.

"You just over did it and you need not to be so hard on yourself." I heard his words but still felt empty and disappointed. I decided to run a hot bath for myself to release the tension I felt. I think I poured the whole bottle of bubble bath in the tub to hide myself under the bubbles. I just wanted to disappear and reappear in a different place.

Once I stepped in the water, tears filled my eyes as if I had just turned on the faucet. Gospel music was playing in the background and entering my spirit. I didn't know that I had more bottled up inside of me than just disappointment. I had been carrying everything on my shoulders and I had the mindset that I needed to always be strong for the family. I felt I had to be this big super wife and super mom. I felt I never needed to show my weaknesses.

I felt if I came down to this level, "the weak way of thinking," then Craig would look down on me as weak. I felt I had no choice now, because Craig was unable to return to his restaurant duties.

I told myself that if I let go of my pains, hurts, and problems, then I would break apart and I wouldn't know how to pick up the pieces again. I found out very quickly once I stepped in the tub that I needed not to be so strong. I found out when my body suddenly went limp, my mind numb and my eyes filled with more tears, a release needed to take place. The more the water filled up in my eyes the harder it was to allow it to flow out.

"I don't know how to cry anymore," I thought to myself. Even though it wasn't a practice of mine to cry, I believed that it would always come naturally. My mind was blocking the very emotions and fighting the tears from coming down. I had to fight with myself and tell myself it was ok to cry.

Self still wasn't listening and fought against me. My mind felt it was going a hundred miles an hour. Finally, I knew what I had to do. I had to confront the source of my pain. I had to go back and remember what made me feel this way in the first place.

Oh my, yes it was Craig and my insecurities. In the beginning of our relationship he made me feel as if I needed to be stronger than what I was. He made me feel that I was weak if I cried, so I needed not to cry. I must admit when we got together I was a wreck.

I was weak and broken, torn from my ex-marriage. Even though Craig and I were together, I still needed to heal. He didn't know or see that in the beginning of our relationship he made it clear to me that he thought he could make me strong from my emotional past. So, he felt by upsetting me from time to time, this would so-call strengthen me. Yet I called it mind games.

He was shocked and couldn't believe that the way he made me feel in the past had such of an effect on me. We sat and talked. As he held me close to comfort me, he made it clear to me that night, he no longer thought with that frame of mind. He assured me that I could cry on his shoulders and he wouldn't look down on me. The relief was there but I still struggled to allow myself to cry in front of him.

Never underestimate true love
06/07/07
10:30 A.M.

Dear Diary

How can you go from a shaky relationship to a good relationship and then back to a shaky one? That may not be a very easy question to answer, but that is what seemed to continue to happen in my relationship. I wanted to be loved and cared for. What was I thinking when I didn't rule out the possibility of getting hurt again? I felt so much for Craig I didn't see that there might be times that he hurt me the same way Brandon did. I just didn't think that he would even try me that way. We had got over all our misunderstandings, I thought. We know each other now, I thought. This man is so unpredictable now that I think about it. He seems to want to challenge me and test me to see if I can handle the pressure. He said he changed his way of thinking about trying to make me strong. I guess not. I told him that he is not the one to make me strong, but God is and he still fails to keep his promise. He was keeping me up all night with his insecurities. He doesn't know how to express himself. Instead he comes out for the attack. Now he reminds me he doesn't trust women as far as he can throw them. He has been around and he swears all women cheat and they all are sluttish and ho's. I said, "oh just because you don't trust women doesn't mean that I am the same as the ones you met." He says, "You are a woman so you are the same." I argued my case, thinking he was out of his mind or trying to tick me off. I told him, "Men can be just as bad but putting me in that category is just wrong." Then he has the nerve to say, "Well that makes you an ex-ho or ex-slut." I just couldn't believe the words that came out of his mouth. I knew that he didn't trust me when he told me this three years ago, but when he called me a slut and a ho, that just hit home with me. It brought back memories of when I was with Brandon and how he would accuse me of cheating on him and call me a "ho." Brandon didn't appreciate me and all he wanted was sex. Then Craig did the most degrading thing and put me back in the bottle I thought was broken in my life. He demands for me to make love to him and if I didn't he could go somewhere else. He was manipulating me every step of the way. About five minutes later I gave in to stop the insults. I jumped on him and I felt numb, I felt as if he had just pulled my heart out and destroyed it. Slowly but surely it got worse as time went on. It felt as if I remained pinned on top of him forever. He continued to ramble on and on about slut's and ho's and not trusting me. I just sunk inside myself and let the tears flow unwillingly from my face, as the knife he had (his words) just kept digging in my heartless chest. He made a new hole over the old scare that had taken so long to heal. He opened the scar right back up, and now I'm feeling I have failed once again. Finally, he feels as if my performance wasn't pleasing and it felt lifeless. I wasn't trying to please him at all, it was peace I desired. I couldn't get off him fast enough. Easing my way off him as quickly as I could, I rolled next to the wall. I couldn't believe it, I had been up sense 2 A.M. and this man wanted to argue. Time seemed to fly because it was five A.M. and he was still fussing under his breath, swearing because I wouldn't say anything else to him. I just felt horrible. I only could do what I knew best and that was to pray a prayer; Lord I don't want my marriage to be like the

last, I can't take another emotional abusive relationship Amen."
Then he makes his way to my side of the bed and demands that
we make love again. It felt as if I just left my body. This man is on
top of me. Is this the man that I love? Why would he want to
make the situation worst by getting his feeling on while my
feelings are lower than low? I was crying and I felt as if I was
drowning in pain, emotionally as he continued. Then I found
enough strength to say, "Get off me" and he says, "Stop your
crying I know I'm not hurting you!" He may have not hurt me
physically but emotionally I was torn. The first thing I thought
was, "This man is just like the last and has put the sour icing on
the cake. How can I forgive him for this?" I just cried and lay
there feeling so dirty and used. I felt like I was back in time and
my husband was not my husband at all, he was acting like a
carbon copy of Brandon at that moment. I felt he was making a
mockery of me and my past hurt. "He doesn't love me, he's using
me and now he has me just where he wants me, in a bottle." I told
myself. When he got done, I ran to the shower, as if to wash away
the pain, shame and emotional hurt I was feeling inside. After
three days of shutting down, I finally concluded....

CHAPTER 12

A DIARY BLOWOUT

8 A.M.

Dear Diary,

When I got up this morning I still felt numb like someone had pushed a needle in my soul and sucked out all my joy of being with this man, my husband and true love. I tell myself that I forgive him but there is still something inside of me that says, "Be aware he's dangerous." He is not violently dangerous, well as far as I know, but emotionally. Now I look at him in a totally different light. You never can expect the unexpected. I don't know what to expect from him and I don't want to let my guard down to find out. He is the man that I trusted with my heart and it appears he only thinks of his himself and his peace of mind. He wanted to make love to me last night and I told him I needed a little time. So, when I was just at the brink of sleep, you know the moment in time where you can't really remember what somebody ask you, or what you may say to them. So, he asked and I think I said yes. I felt him inside of me and I really felt angry. Yet for some reason I went into a deeper sleep. I don't remember anything else. I don't know if he stopped or if he finished, but I do know I didn't want to be there, so my mind must have shut off and sleep was on my side. This morning he was still being extra nice to me. So, I would give him a smile or two, yet he still knew I wasn't happy. I can still feel his testing aspect, as he's simply testing me to see if I still loved him. Back to this morning, I noticed he would throw a little, "baby can you iron my clothes for me?" in a nice sweet voice. Then throw in, "oh I want to see your sexy body as you iron my clothes" making growling noises as if he was turned on by me or trying to turn me on. Well it didn't work. Yet I went ahead and ironed his clothes and walked him to the door. But something inside of me felt a relief when I didn't have to look him in the face and feel bad. He said sorry to me twice more as he walked out of the door. He blew sorry kisses to my virginal parts, knowing that he took advantage of me and then again for hurting me emotionally. He gave me a warm hug and a kiss on the noise and then my mouth, as he turned and walked out the door. I tried to embrace the hug and kisses but I continued to feel the wall that I placed up, which blocked my emotions to him. "I just want to be happy." I kept telling myself. Yet he continues to feel as if he must break the trail of happiness in our marriage by hurting me and adding arguments or disagreements every six months to supposedly keep us normal.

He said to me once, "If we never argue then we wouldn't be as close because we have to have some type of makeup time or an emotional strengthening mechanism." I didn't agree, nor did I understand what he was talking about. I felt he was just scared to embrace the love I was giving him and the joy that followed.

06/09/07
9:36 A.M.

Dear Diary,

I had another long night last night. When he got home yesterday I wanted to talk to him about how he had hurt me. So, I needed to let him know how bad he made me feel. I wanted him to see from my eyes and find out why he would do such a thing. We started talking about what caused him to act like he did in the first place. He tells me it was because I mentioned it would be cool *if we experienced the Reality Show "Wife Swap" and maybe pick up, fifty thousand dollars in the process. I could tell he really didn't want anything to do with it, but he joked around with me and acted as if he was interested. So, I called the lady for an application. When the lady called me back and sent me an application, the truth was revealed. So now he is so upset, (remember he didn't say anything to me about why or what) but that's when the ugly things came from his mouth. "Get out the room, why don't you go sleep in the living room? Don't touch me; I don't want you touching me." You would think that would be enough of his evil ways. I asked him, "What is your reason for not telling me straight up that you didn't want to do it. He said, 'I can't tell you nothing." I heard this often or every time we had a disagreement. He plays this mean role to hurt me blocking my words. He has insecurity issues and turned the whole idea of the show around to a cheating situation. He also said he didn't need anyone coming in his home telling him what he needed to change because everything was fine the way it was. I had a feeling that he wouldn't go for it but that one percent chance always over takes me. I just wanted to see what his view would be and if he would give it a chance. I wanted to see if he would maybe take a chance on anything that would be out of the ordinary and have that opportunity to get us out of the rut we were in. He wouldn't though, and he says he never will. In his mind, he tells me he is always trying to please me, not himself. I don't know what kind of pleasing he is trying to do with his crazy demonstration. He hurts me, expecting me to get over the hurt like it never happened. If I don't get over it in twenty-four to forty-eight hours then he makes an off the wall comment like this, "maybe it was a mistake to marry you." I am starting to believe that this is his true feelings because he acts as if he's not happy anymore. Then he say's what I thought I would never hear come out of his mouth, "I only* married you to please you." I questioned myself as to why he continues to throw daggers with his words. I began to feel he enjoyed hurting me. Then he has the nerve to say, "Let's make love." What kind of twisted mind did he have for him to continue to play around with my emotions like I was his fool? So of course, I allowed him to make love to me and in his head my night of pain he caused was over. During the whole time we made love, all I could do was cry. I told him, "I want my marriage and I always did and it is so sad to know you never wanted it in the first place." My mind continued to think about the boys. Then I started to encourage myself and tell myself, "Ok, if this is what he wants to do, then I needed to let him go." I don't know where his head was but he really wanted to rub in the situation. He says he didn't want to wait ten years, then down the road a divorce; so, it would be better if we did it sooner than later. I have heard all these words before from him but what hurts the most is, most likely, this is the truth. I love him so much and I will pray for him. It hurts to know that the man you love and want to spend the rest of your life with, gives up every time there's a disagreement. He gives up if it is not in his comfort zone and yet tries to please me under a lie to keep my mouth shut. What can I do and what can I say when you know that your second marriage may be a lie as well? You trusted this man with your heart, your kid's heart and now he states he doesn't want what he has vowed for. He is living a lie now and I am living a nightmare. I am living a prayer that I prayed would never come to pass. I didn't want to live with my new husband and feel trapped and misunderstood. I wanted my marriage to last. I didn't want to be together for three years and married a year, for my past to be repeated all over again. Brandon and I were married one year and all hell broke loose. I love my husband and I am just going to ask God to take me by the hand and carry our marriage through. Only God have the power to change his heart.

He may feel as if he has made a mistake, and feel it's better to leave or give up, but I pray that God gives him the vision to see that life is a struggle. I really do believe that God had a hand in our marriage and allowed it to take place. I don't feel as if it is a mistake. I pray for understanding and better communication, so our marriage will not be based on past experiences and past pains. I pray that God will deliver us both from our fears and hurts, bonding us together to make this marriage work. I wanted this marriage from the very beginning and I will not let the devil destroy it over some of my weaknesses or his weaknesses. No matter what Craig may say to me, or how he tries to use his fears against me, or how he may try to use my weaknesses to make him strong; I will not let his insecurities destroy me. I am a child of God and He is my strength. So, my marriage may seem to be on shaky ground right now, but God has something in store for the both of us. I will not let a little or what I may feel to be a lot of emotional pains to take my focus off the promise God has for me. To be successful in my marriage and career is what I pray for and is what I will go after.

06/11/07
6:45 A.M.

Dear Diary,

I went to church yesterday expecting to hear a word from God and that's exactly what I got and then some. God gave me more than what I expected. I was delivered from the lie the devil told me about my marriage. With that I see a whole new light. A piece of me felt like I was going in circles and my pain and afflictions were out to get me. I didn't feel like I was strong enough to go through the storm and to face my discretions. Now I see that the devil thought he had me and he thought that I was too weak. The devil thought that God wasn't going to give me the direction that I had been praying for, as my Pastor stated, "He must not know me, for I am a child of the highest God." I am his daughter and he is going to move my mountains and whatever afflictions and discretions that the devil think he has a hold on, well I am not going to let him no longer take my joy. I am strong and I am blessed because God loves me and I don't need anyone to tell me that I can't do anything or that I am not qualified to do something. I am just that qualified because I have God on my side and I am not going to give up. My husband and I were having a dispute about goals and dreams. Just because he knows me to be a certain way, he may feel I am not capable of doing things that will cost my time and money. He feels I should live life on a day-to-day base. I told him that I am not going to give up my dreams and goals because I have failed in a few. I have God on my side and that is more reason enough for me to press forward for what God has in store for me. This is just what the devil would tell my husband, "You shouldn't support your wife for when she fails, she will blame you." I couldn't allow the devil to get the glory. "No, I am going to go after my dreams because if I don't, I will never know the true blessings that are in store for me," I yelled to the devil. The devil thinks if he destroys our marriage or throw darts at me, then I will run away again. Well the devil doesn't know that I am changed and God is my strong tower. I will not run away from my marriage this time. I am going to continue to pray over my marriage and lift it up in the name of Jesus. "You can't have my marriage devil, it is mine and God gave it to me and I will fight to keep it; for God is on my side and he will fight my battles." I declared.

06/14/07
8:25 A.M.

Dear Diary,

This week has really been a blessing because God opened my eyes through the pain and let me see. I came to understand that with understanding comes more love. The more I love my husband and God, the stronger our relationship has become. God has given me more than I can give life itself and that is true love. I now know that true love defeats all fear and without fear, my life is selfless and full of more love. I thank God for being the author and finisher of my faith. God will allow me to accomplish my dreams and keep my marriage. Last night we made love and talked as we do. We like to communicate to each other in the mist of making love. When you can talk to each other in a venerable state I feel this is a place you can really reach your partner. They have their heart open, ears and maybe eyes open and they can truly hear what you must say, whether it was nice or not so nice. I love my husband and we are going to have our ups and downs and maybe some disagreements, but I am sticking it out till the end. God has truly blessed me with this person who understands me (sometimes) but knows what I want. He tries to please me in any way he possibly knows how. He knows the side of me to keep me happy, and we can learn to help each other with our weaknesses. He has helped me learn to get over things and not hold on to the past, creating anger. He has helped me know that you can get your point across without nagging. If a man wants to listen they will. No matter how loud you scream or yell; if they don't want to listen to you or give you the time of day, then they won't. You can't make them by trying to over-power them.

10/7/07
10:20 P.M.
Four months later

Dear Diary,

I sit here in the living room thinking how a man that you love so much could constantly push you away. He has his ways of pushing me away when things are going well when we are getting closer. I love this man so much and the more I love him, the more I see that love seems to frighten him and me a little too. I want to get inside of his head and read all his thoughts sometimes. Sometimes I want to view his thoughts of why he's so angry and takes it out on me.

He now has accused me of cheating on him because I have experienced some irritation, but I have always experienced some type of irritation. He then finds change in the sofa and says, "Who have you had in our home and what man has been sitting here?" He goes on to say that he knows I don't sit on the couch, so it must have been a man. I told him, "Yes it was a man, YOU!" I don't know for the most part but he keeps tearing at my heart. I just try to rub it off and move on with life. This feeling of coldness has been a couple of days but the feelings of resentment have been a least a month. Just last month he just ups and packs his clothes and says he's leaving, breaking my heart again. Giving me some crazy explanation that he needs to leave because he is again holding me back or I would be better off with somebody younger. Then after a while he gives me another excuse that he holds things in and for the last six months there *have been some things that has been eating away at him. He says it's difficult to hold conversations with me or give me advice about anything because he believes I have the mindset that I already know everything. That is not true but I can't seem to win him over on that point. Whatever is truly bothering him he's struggling with identifying the real problem. When I do want to express myself, I find myself babbling. I think I tend to think faster than what I allow to come out of my mouth. So, therefore I don't ever really get my point across. I came to him and asked him, "Why do you continue to push me away?" He refuses to answer. I just didn't understand how every six months or so, he could continue to pull away and push the one that loves you away. Yet, whether he realizes it or not, it tends to tug at your soul. I have tried to let go all the times he has continued to push me away but every time he does it, it leaves me with a lasting impressing. I feel that one day he just might walk out and I am not aware of how I will deal with it. Sorry to say, but sometimes I just wished he had of left the last time he packed because then I wouldn't anticipate its coming. I feel I must be forever ready to feel the terrible heartache that he puts me through repeatedly, for nothing. I want to not feel the threat or the fear that he will leave me. You see he knows I fear it and dread it, so I think he plays at my emotions to keep his mind at ease. It also forces me into a world of my own to protect my heart. I must hold back the tears and trust that happiness is not a world away but a world I already have. I know my career in the Criminal Justice field is going to take off and with only two and a half years left before I get my AA, I just know God has something in store for us. I really do wonder about Craig though because he really is Night and Day. I never know when his drama is going to hit me but when it does, he makes it so dramatic. I may write to ease the pain and the pressure of the tears but it has left one more scare on the depth of my heart.*

The year 2007 was filled with so much confusion and uncertainty. I didn't know if our marriage would last to see the year 2008 yet alone 2009. I just hoped and prayed that this man that was in my life would someday understand that love was there for him.

I wanted happiness for him and the more ups and downs we went through, the more I saw how afraid of the love he was. I know love is what he wanted. The fear of truly indulging in love and enjoying the life that God has given us was still a continual fight. Craig has told me a lot of things; he practically forced me to cry because of his painful tactics.

It caused scars that are still healing to this day. Through all of this we both have caused pain, but God is the one who blessed us with one another.

You may be reading this and may wonder, "How could he be this good man when he caused so much pain?" Well sometimes men and women can still be good to one another inflicting pain on one another to ease their own pains and fears.

I feel when a person is free from the hurts of their past, then they will be able to enjoy the love of their future. I can see the hurt, fear, and anger that he was dealing with from within. He may have had his outburst every six months but in the meantime, he was treating me like a queen and his children came first. Therefore, I fight for my marriage that God has given me. Each day, month and year that past I notice a change. I notice it is not as frequent as six months; it has gone past the expected outbreak. He is more aware that he has a problem now and tries to communicate it before pointing the unnecessary blame.

We still have our ups and our downs, our disagreements and our agreements but what is more important? I always tell him no matter how mad or disappointed I may be for a time, I only have so much time in one day.

I want to enjoy all the time I have with him on a happy note. I would love to take the moments of pain, anger, being confused, being afraid and make them disappear. Life is too short to dwell on the things you cannot change and the people that may or may not change.

You must be able to change yourself and strive for joy within yourself and through whatever you have your faith in. Fear, pain, and people can either make you or break you, so we must keep our eyes on the promise. My husband has not broken me but God has made me a stronger person. Through all the pain, God was the one there mending all the pieces back together again.

So, the year 2007 is gone and the year 2008 is now a focus. Craig hasn't had the time to focus too much on his fears but they do seem to pop up from time to time.

So, I knew after a long year, all the pain, anxiety and fears that had built a resting place in me over the years, had to be released. I still had a problem getting all my mixed emotions out, for I knew my struggles with getting the career I wanted wasn't over. I still had two more chances to complete and pass the test and I knew worrying about old feelings from the past would only hold me back. I began to pray and ask the Lord again for strength in my time of need. I knew if I failed a second time our income would be gone. I knew that Craig was still unable to work and I felt I needed to do my best to pass the test and get this job.

The test was three weeks away and it couldn't have come quicker. In the meantime, God opened doors for us to move in a three-bedroom two-bath home with wood floors and a back yard. He allowed us to move into just what I had prayed for.

The move was a success but the funds were just enough to pay the bills as they came. Test time had arrived and I just knew God wouldn't leave me or forsake me. "I studied the information, so the test wouldn't be a problem," I told myself. I once again went through the test process and had to wait a week for the results. The day of the results, Craig and I lay in the bed having a conversation. Craig mentioned out of the blue "I guess I will have to make appointments to make love to you?" I couldn't believe what I was hearing, for I knew he was about to start one of his off the wall disagreements.

I asked him what did he mean and he stated, "Well you are always sleeping now, I can't remember the last time we made love." He knew I wasn't used to working night shift, and the desire for him never left.

My mind was going fast and in circles, for I couldn't believe this man was picking with me about sex. I could barely keep my eyes open after twelve hours and he expects me to, "what" come home and ride him until the sun comes up? I started to have mixed feelings about how he truly felt about me getting the job. I had worked so hard and felt kind of upset. I had struggled and worked my butt off to make sure we kept a roof over our heads and he's tripping about sex. I couldn't believe it, for he knew I was always about pleasing my man but after a long night of working, I truly had sleep on the brain.

I told him that there wasn't a need for an appointment. It was ridicules for him to even think such a thing. I asked him what he wanted me to do since he felt this way. I just knew he had some smart remark up his sleeve.

"Are you going to masturbate, leave me, cheat on me, what will it be?" I was throwing all the questions out there. I was so tired of his petty mind games. He just responded with his favorite phrase "Whatever" to end the disagreement. After a few minutes of silence, he says, "Are you going to see if you passed?" At that moment, I had my back to him and my face to the wall. I was silently crying with one tear at a time rolling down my check. I had mixed feelings and I said to myself, "If this job is going to change him for the worst, I might not need it." I no longer had hope of having a passing score at that moment.

I was basically willing to give it all up at that very moment to keep peace and happiness. I wanted our marriage to be as peaceful as a marriage should be and if something of this world was trying to divide it, I was willing to let it go.

I jumped out of the bed quickly to conceal the tears that was flowing out of my eyes. I slowed my pace as I walked down the hall into the living room where our computer was. My heart pounded as I pulled up the results to find out our fate. Lord and behold the results read "FAILED" in big red bold letters. This time I wasn't sad or mad but numb inside not knowing what to think first. I walked back into the room and got back into the bed where Craig was still laying. I then said to him "I hope you are happy, I FAILED and you can get all the sex you want." He was shocked when I told him and a little saddened for me, for his voice became soft and comforting.

He reached over to touch me with his big warm hands, signaling to me that he was sorry. I continued to stare at the wall as if I didn't feel his touch. I mentioned to him, "Now it is me and you, since I have to resign immediately."

I confided in him telling him the process of the company letting me go and how I only had one more shot to be rehired and pass the test. I then asked him if he still felt the need to make an appointment with me because if he did I wouldn't even go back for the third test. He then grabbed me and held me close, telling me he was truly sorry and he didn't want me to give up on what I had worked so hard for. We then agreed that we would work harder to satisfy each other's needs. The only problem or I guess solution in a way was I no longer had a job to tire me out. The next day I was required to immediately place in my resignation and return all loaned property.

It felt like a piece of me was stripped away, as I handed over the items. I signed my letter, for the chance to return within six months for rehire. I didn't want to give up and I knew deep down inside this job was my goal. I felt when the next test came I would give it my all once again. Craig never complained after that about getting him some. He fell right back into his role of supporting me while I prepared again for the third and final test. I had one month to prepare and I still felt as if I had let the family down. Once again, I was in the rat race trying to find closure and a new job to support the family. I put in at least fifty applications over the Internet and got two bites that went nowhere. I felt desperate, left without a paddle floating alone in the muck.

I began to feel depressed within myself, not wanting to do anything around the house or deal with anyone. My mind kept saying, "Go back to work, support, support, support." Craig began to see my determination to find a job and tells me maybe I should just wait. "I had been waiting," I thought and I didn't want to wait any longer.

The discussion of bills never ended and I, "Superwoman" felt the need to step it up, to keep her man from stressing. I decided to take a job at a telemarketing company to get a few bills paid. It took three weeks to get one hundred and nineteen dollars. I was frustrated and angry but still the money came in time to pay another unexpected bill. After that ordeal, I decided to wait on the Lord to be rehired and focus on the test at hand; so, I gave up the job. I had no time to waste, for this was my last chance.

If I blew this one, I would have to start from the drawing board. Now that I wasn't working, we were struggling all over again. The rent was behind by a month but I told Craig, "Let's not worry because God always has made a way."

Even in the mist of our faith the devil would try to get me off track with little thoughts that ran through my head. Little thoughts like, "You're a failure and your whole family will end up on the streets." I shook my head to get the negative thoughts out as quickly as they came. I called charity after charity to see if we could get some help and I received no answer. Just when I about gave in God opened the door. Not one but two charities finally answered and paid our rent for two months including the light bill. I gave God all the praise, for I knew without trusting in him, the bills would not have been paid. Our struggles were not over yet but by the grace of God he was still on our side.

Craig and I had not disagreed or had an argument while we went through this trying time. We remained one another's comfort and friend.

We continued to hold each other up, expecting nothing but God's unconditional grace. I asked Craig if he was up to going back to work since he was feeling a lot better now and I still had a few weeks before the test.

Craig agreed to go back to work, even though we both knew it was only a matter of time before the government stepped in and took the money he owed. Whether it was child support or back taxes we both knew his check wouldn't be much of nothing but every little penny helped.

The time came for me to take the final and last test that would determine our fate and future. I prayed and totally gave it to God, "For if it is for me Lord, it will be for me." I prayed. A week later after taking the test the results were in. I walked slowly to my computer and pulled up the results.

Covering the screen, I felt my stomach bubble, as the results were revealed right behind the covering of my hand.

My heart was pounding, I felt like it was about to jump out of my chest. Finally, I slowly took my hand off the screen and I saw, "PASS" in big bold red letters. I screamed and jumped all over the house in excitement as if I had won the lotto. I couldn't believe I was done. All the challenging work, long night studies, body aches and headaches, it all had finally paid off. I now eight months later had the keys to my future. I just needed to be rehired. The test of our faith was being tried again for it took another two months to be rehired. My faith was still set on trusting God.

When it felt like the recruiter wasn't moving fast enough to rehire me, the money had gone. Everything was past due and the rent came faster it seems than any other bill.

Just when I was about to make the call to the landlord explaining our situation, a letter came in the mail. I couldn't believe what I was reading, for it was another bail out plain God had in store for us.

To our surprise but sadden to read, the landlord himself was having troubles and the house we lived in was being foreclosed on. The thoughts ran through our head "we have to move again." The disappointment of never having the opportunity to buy what we thought would be a magnificent home for the family, had come to an end. So, we talked to the landlord and no more money was required for the remaining time we lived in the home. He decided to squash the rent we owed and gave us a two-month deadline. You see God was still giving us the grace we had prayed for. Look at God!

We agreed once again to leave the home the way he gave it to us, as we went on our search for another place. In the mist of all the confusion and money problems, Craig suddenly becomes ill after one month of working. He was diagnosed with a virus called, "Bale's Palsy" a virus that takes over the nerves in the brain, face and throat, which can temporarily paralyze them.

CHAPTER 13

THE TRANSITION

God was testing our faith repeatedly. He wanted to see just how much we would lean and depend on him. Not one time during our ups and downs did I throw in Craig's face; he was responsible for getting us out of the mess we were in. I've learned over the years that it is hard enough for a man to just be a man.

There could be some unpaid bills weighing on his shoulders keeping his spirits down. It could be child support, back taxes, the pressure of moving all the time or even the cost of a new child.

Either way, if he says he's the man, then most likely he will try to do whatever he can to take care of the family. Hopefully legally!

He may be struggling to support a family that he wants to protect. The man is always trying to demonstrate he's the man. He has the desire to give his wife the world but is constantly reminded of the debt that is weighing him down. He needs encouragement, love, support and yes money.

If all don't fail but the money is just not there, then we as their help mate should give whatever else that can be given such as love, support, respect and maybe, just a little space.

When you have a good man, or want a good man, women in general should stop placing unreachable demands on the man. Men can retain so much in their minds but if you give them a chance they will try to hold the world in their hands.

DEMANDING A MAN

A man never wants to feel as though his wife will nag him all day every day. We as women and some men may feel that nagging is a form of instruction. Well ladies and gentlemen words to the wise, nagging is nagging and they don't hear anything we say but blaw, blaw, and blaw. What are we nagging for anyway when we can do just what they can do? So, we may complain; "they are not taking out the trash." Then why aren't you taking out the trash? Did they take out the trash before they moved in with you? Did they take out the trash at their momma's house?

So, you continue to complain; "they didn't check the air in my tires, check the oil, wash my car or give me multiple orgasms all week long. Oh by the way they need to work seven days a week and come home and hold a lengthy conversation with you too."

All of this you can do. Ok, exception of the multiple orgasms. We as women place in our demands and when they don't get met, we feel the man is no good. Ladies and gentlemen don't get me wrong. This is not excusing the lazy, dead beat men that don't hold up their own pants and women that don't hold down their skirts.

Also, this includes the women that may feel that they don't have an obligation as well in the relationship, other than to look good. I don't speak to excuse those that may feel as if the world should be handed to them on a platter. I don't excuse the people that don't give a care about anyone but himself or herself, showing nothing but selfishness.

Those are the ones that don't deserve you. If you are the opposite of them and truly want something in life, then love will find you.

All we should want is for one another to do what is right. There are roles for the woman and the man in a relationship. It should paint a picture that; there is responsibility in the relationship to share. We as women shouldn't try to take the entire load on our plate, and then complain about help. If he is willing and able, then there should be a sense of togetherness throughout the home.

We should be helpmates one to another; acknowledging what God has placed us together to accomplish. There shouldn't be catfights, nagging and pulling of hair but a willing heart to work as a team.

When this has been established, then working together as a team will not be so hard. If she takes out the trash one day, he shouldn't just wash his hands of the job but thank her for her help.

If he washes the dishes one day, she shouldn't stop, but appreciate his help and consideration and tell him so. A team will be born and together happiness can grow. Choosing to be in a relationship should mean; the questions have already been asked. What am I talking about?

Well most of us, including myself, forget that we can ask as many questions as we want before we get involved with someone. To learn who a person is, you must ask questions.

For example, questions like; what do they feel their role is in the relationship? How can we work together to make things smooth? Do you like to clean? Do you pay your bills? What kind of debt do you have? These should not be asked after moving forward. For you might get a rude of awakening.

In knowing this you will know first-hand, if they are honest and what to expect.

So, in knowing all of this I never said that a woman doesn't need a man. In wanting a man, I know from being a woman that I can tend to be demanding. I have used my demands and made them seem they were requirements.

Which can turn into demands and the demands eventually turns into an argument or a nag.

Men barely like to talk. What makes you think that they want to argue with you too? Women can have a mindset that we need to get the point across either quickly or directly.

Men are not our children and I feel that we are automatically built with a motherly tone and an instinct to give demands. This can be a gift and a curse that can be self-taught to control it.

We just must recognize the right person to give demands to (children or in a job if necessary). I believe that just because it is built in us, doesn't make it right to use it on our man. A man might stay in the home with you physically but can leave mentally. He may sleep in the same bed with you, come home after work, but his mind is still not there.

He may share certain conversations with you but change the subject often, because in his mind he doesn't want to be there.

He may want peace and gratitude. He wants to come home to a "hay honey how was your day, what can I do for you" now and then.

I know a lot of you are probably thinking, "What planet is she on?" Well I am on planet happiness, peace and love with a good man, in the working. I work hard every day to make him happy and keep peace in the home.

Yes, there will be days we have our ups and downs and our disagreements but the good days have truly outweighed the bad. Remember Craig has had his moments every six to 8 months that lasted maybe one to three days.

So, while it may have taken me a little bit to get over the incidents, that is still only twice a year. I can't complain and I can't really hold anything against him for having his moments, I too have had mine.

What I have learned is; if a person has done you wrong, they should have acknowledged their wrong. They should make a mend and do what they can to change their ways or change their actions to avoid the same problem in the future.

It has been a long journey for Craig and I, and we still have even longer to go. I plan to see the future. Whatever it takes for me to make this marriage work in God's eyes, I am going to do my best.

You may have asked the question earlier; what do I mean about working hard to keep him? You may say, "Shouldn't it just work if they really want it to?" Well we all know this is wishful thinking and not reality. Happiness comes and goes quicker than love. Happiness is based on happenings. Love is a choice that we make between one another.

When you truly know the definition behind love it becomes so much more powerful. Love will always outweigh lust. If love is truly there, it will carry you through the good and the bad. Love should be given without regard, but is selfless.

When a person gives love and the other receives it, then the one on the receiving end is supposed to return the love back one hundred percent. Love is more than the words "I love you" but love is actions. It's kind of like touching it to believe it. It's not how much she or he can give me but how much can we give each other. Again, I believe love is a choice; an agreement between two individuals that chose to become more than one sided. When you chose to take on that other person as a companion or mate, then you have just chosen to become a part of them and them apart of you.

We enter a world that is confused about the true meaning of love but it can be defined. If you can't seem to wrap your minds around it, then think of love like a jigsaw puzzle.

At first you were lost and it was confusing but you continued to work the puzzle and with no instruction you seem to master it. You mastered it because you worked at it and didn't give up. You didn't cheat to get the answers, nor did you fight yourself to solve the puzzle. You mastered it eventually and because challenging work paid off the puzzle was complete. We have all the tools we need to get an understanding of each other; all we need to do is communicate.

Communication is the key; not arguing, yelling, screaming or fighting the person. Harsh words and physical abuse is not going to get the message across male or female.

We must be able to think about what we are truly trying to say before the words are spoken. Words can slip as we say; "out of our mouths" but you can't slip them back in once they have been spoken. Our words are vital to the survival of your relationship. Stop trying to read each other's minds. What is truly needed is sometimes for someone to just stop talking and listen.

Before you try to truly get an understanding of what is going on inside someone else's head, you need to know what is going on in your own head. You need to find out who you truly are. You may think to yourself, "what does finding out "who" you are have to do with a relationship?" Well, it has everything to do with a relationship and much more.

You should try to identify who you are before getting involved in a relationship. Sometimes we want people to change for us but we must be willing to change as well. We may not be able to completely please someone to the fullest but you can make the road a little smoother.

I have now realized that the people we may be in love with are forever changing. Our looks, wants, desires and dreams. We change on a day-to-day basis; never thinking or considering the next change that may take place. We can want or expect our mates to become accustomed to what has changed, not realizing the impact. Sometimes it becomes overwhelming for either person, when each party must be willing to wait for the other to adjust to it. The key is giving that person the suitable amount of time to adjust.

By getting to know who you are; you will begin to find yourself learning from yourself every day. You will be able to look at your own changes or flaws and keep them in check.

Doing this keeps the pressure off your mate to try to figure you out. In my opinion, the worse thing my husband could say to me when it came to communication was "I don't understand you; you are a hard person to get along with." We should want a clear path of understanding as well as communication.

HONESTY AND TRUST

There's nothing better than knowing you have an honest relationship and nothing worse than knowing you have a liar for a man or woman. We want to feel that we can share our heart-felt secrets and love with this person. We want to know that the love we give is received and given genuinely.

We want to be able to trust them with our love, heart and future. We want to know that life will not be a waste if we choose to spend the rest of our life with this person. We do desire these things, but if we don't ask the right questions in the beginning, then we can't expect for everything great to fall in our laps.

The truth can be far-fetched for some people and the words "I love you" can be an effortless way of not telling the truth. They can be willing to lie, cheat, and steal just to keep a pigment of this world and you in their world. Then you may say, "why not just tell the truth and become an honest person?" It's easier said than done. If they are not exposed to the truth in some shape or form, the depiction of a lie can seem like the truth; even if a person has been deceived as a child or even as an adult, then lying can feel normal to them.

There are a lot of signs given before and during a relationship of how honest a person will be. I am not saying that there are not some people out there that can't fool you, because they lied well. No, I truly believe that there are people that have made telling lies a career.

I also believe that majority of the time, we as women ignore the signs thinking we can change them or believe they will just change overnight. We settle because we blame "LOVE," then we are unhappy when things began to fall apart. How do we avoid getting hurt or falling for the lies and untruth? How do we find happiness and keep it? Well we need to stop looking.

If you are a woman stop looking everywhere for Mr. Right at the clubs, malls, stores and bars and even church. I didn't say stop desiring Mr. Right, but when you as a woman look for a man, then you are messing up the order of God.

God has someone for all of us and we must ask him to bring us the right one for us. You can ask God for just what you want and if you believe in him, he will give you the desires of your heart. There's a scripture that says, "A man who finds a wife finds a good thing and obtains favor from the Lord." Prov. 18:22 (Holman's Student Bible)

I don't recall seeing it the other way around. You might say, well I don't believe in that. Ok, I can't fight you on that one but have you ever wondered why we keep finding the wrong one? God has someone for everyone even if it's just for a season in your life.

We must be ready to keep our eyes open to see when they are there. The love will come, the trust will come but true honesty must be planted in your soul.

COMMITMENT

Commitment comes in many different forms for a woman. Some women may feel a simple commitment with him just by him saying, "I love you." Some feel that living together can be a since of commitment. Having sex all the time, partying together etc.... There could be numerous of things to make it appears commitment is there. Truly what is commitment? The dictionary states, "to promise, pledge, vow, obligation, assurance, binder, dedication and loyalty" are defined. Is this what your man or woman is showing towards you? Are these things being demonstrated to you in your relationship?

These things are all commitments and can't be separated if it's true commitment. Is he or she willing to go the mile or the long hall for you? If the answer is yes, then being there a future of marriage if you're single?

Is this person willing to be selfless enough to commit to what he or she has said they are committed to for the rest of their life? You might get a lot of blank stares or no answers at all. The phrase "rest of your life" just might have scared them. It shouldn't, I would think but life has a way of distorting the very meaning of marriage and commitment.

Just say life is truly happy for you and you have everything you think you desire, the love of your life, children, career, and your health.

You've prayed for God to send you this man or woman of your dreams to complete your life's circle. You now feel that God has done just that but suddenly, your world is turned upside down because your soul mate's changes.

He begins to express to you his unhappiness with himself and his health. He's unhappy with his inability to give you and the kids the world. He begins to express these feelings in a manner he is almost at a loss for words.

He's no longer happy and thinks if he leaves it would be better off for the family. He no longer wants the responsibility of staying home and tending to the house, like a woman in his eyes. On the other hand, he has a genuine love for you and the kids and is willing to stay if that will make the family happy.

He's at a crossroad with himself and his family. He has been the ideal man the whole time you have been together, now this. You say to yourself, "it hasn't been long enough because a number in years can't give you the lifelong happiness you desired."

Now that you know your husband is in pain, unhappy and wants to give up, what do you do? What can you do that you haven't already done? I feel the only thing to do is pray for him and continue to love him whole-heartedly.

This man that I speak of is my husband. He had anger and anxiety of not being able to do for his family after coming down with his illness of Bale's Palsy. I love this man with all my heart, but men have a built-in obligation from the beginning of time to fulfill their duties. Men have the duties to protect, love and provide. If they feel they have failed even one, then they can and will walk away from it all when it gets overwhelming. We as their women should be more understanding of whatever struggles they may face within themselves.

A man only knows what a woman tells him about herself, but if that man has a sense of emotional awareness he can pick up exactly what is wrong with that woman and how she would feel, even if she never brings it up. A man can feed off a woman's emotions and her weaknesses.

He knows how to play a game the woman has mastered. He knows how to wait for the right moment and then may pick and nit at her to get her in a place of submission. A man knows if he has a strong woman and even if she has some weaknesses, he will be able to see that she will one day be able to stand on her feet again, with or without him. A man wants a woman to be strong in mind and spirit but never overbearing.

If he works with her to lift her up and appreciates her, then she would be in his corner until the day he dies. If a man has the mindset that he must keep a woman in her place and feels she is beneath him, then he will do whatever he can to keep her down.

He may hurt her to keep her under his power or control. Men can be unpredictable, and some of them like to keep it that way to keep women wondering what might happen. He may give her enough time to heal from the last hurt and pain he put her through, just to keep her from leaving him. If a man has the idea that he is the one to keep her in his control and it is his duty to make her this stronger woman, then he feels he is molding her. What he is unaware of; resentment may be building up in her.

She might forgive him but she will not forget the pain and how he makes her feel. He is also unaware that there is only a matter of time before she puts up a wall against him completely and he will be in the dark from her emotionally and mentally.

The happy go lucky woman he once knew will become mean and angry towards him. She may still please her man because that is built inside of her to do, but she will fail to give him the affection that he longs for. He will not understand that he is the cause of what he has created. If he realizes that she is this way because of him and she despises him and his every action, then he might change his ways. Maybe he will make it before she has changed her mind to stay. In her mind, she may have decided that she can't take it anymore and she must free herself for her to see happiness.

If he makes it in time then there is a chance that he can save his marriage or relationship with her. She will forgive him if she has a forgiving heart, but she now must go through a spiritual deliverance.

Only God can heal her hurt and pain that she has packed away repeatedly inside of her. She's lost inside of her own emotions and she's crying out for someone to save her. She wants to be rescued more so by her man that she loves so dearly. She will allow him to get close to her heart repeatedly seeking the reconciliation of her relationship.

She's an open book and wants him to read the pages of her book to get the answers to her insecurities and fears. If he never communicates to her and attacks her again and again with his fears, emotions and past experiences, then she will never get her book read.

They will both be in the dark on each other's pain and emotional struggles. How can we go through life with a person and not communicate the things that hurt us the most to the person we love? It's so amazing how easily we attack one another instead of lifting each other up.

We expect things to go our way and when they don't we act like children and pout and cry expecting to get our way through a tantrum.

Once we see and understand, then we can pick ourselves up and try to help them before they give up. We must be willing to do what we can to help them but keeping in mind they are the ones to fulfill their own destiny.

All the sex or money in the world will not make a man feel totally complete. I believe the number one cause for divorce is money, kids and no communication. Many relationships go out the window because the women have kids that the men don't want, "as if she became pregnant by herself," or both share kids that they can't agree on.

The money is a major division that continues to divide homes. It can be more bills than money, more debt and no money or too much money and no love. There has become less desire to stick out the struggle but more running away to solve nothing.

Happy homes can continue to be happy homes if one of the two or both doesn't give up. When one gives up, it can bring a division or separation in the relationship and home.

It causes arguments that were never there, but now is. It causes the strife and stresses that the children will have to endure. These things will take place because somebody or both decided to throw in the towel.

Love and a good relationship can happen, so don't doubt it. Having a true soul mate is possible, even if you don't see the future. We expect so much right now and can miss our future right now. God knows the outcome even when we feel all is lost.

God can mend a broken heart even when we can't. The problem is we try to do it all on our own and we fail. We try to fix problems that our husband or wife may have and we end up making it worse. There's a scripture I truly believe and it says, "Trust in the Lord with all your heart, and do not rely on your own understanding." Prov. 3:5 (Holman's Student Bible)

I have been through a long journey and you now know the road that I have traveled but this is not the end of my road. I don't know if Romeo and Juliet (Craig and I) will stay happily ever after forever. I don't know if we both will find the answers to the problems we may face in the future. What I do know is "Love" is patient and love is kind, love does not envy: is not boastful: is not conceited." I Cor. 13:4 (Holman's Student Bible)

No matter what, I will continue to put my trust in God. I will continue to live in Gods eyesight, serving him all the days of my life. God will surly bless me in my faithfulness. God will never leave us or forsake us. All we must do is come to him with all our hearts. He can mend the broken hearts and give you a new love. He will make you feel like a new person.

He can because I am a witness to becoming a new person in Christ. We must learn to love, love to learn and forgive along the way. Doing this will bring blessings your way and your true love will come too.

If you live right according to Gods word, gifts will be established in heaven as it is on earth.

So, the answer to some of the horrible ordeals you may have experienced in your relationship is: you must be willing to work together.

If you have the higher power to lean on then He will be the strength of the relationship when you feel you can't work together. You also must practice having a mindset that is free of negative thoughts or anger. We must understand that our minds can be like tapes.

If you pull and tug on them repeatedly, the tape can break. Our minds must be free of stress and worries no matter how much we feel we have everything under control.

There is a breaking point in all of us that we don't want to reach. We need to learn ourselves. So, if we can't reach the mind of our love one, we will be able to reach ourselves. We have the power to change our own situation through prayer and by standing on the Word of God, knowing that what you believe is not something unattainable.

We must never underestimate that the devil can trick our minds crazy and that the person or persons around us do have an impact on us. If we don't have a higher power that we trust in and have faith in, then you should examine what you live for. Is it you're children, husband, yourself, your parents, or successful life?

Will this strength be able to keep you when you have fallen? We were not placed on this earth to be abused, misused or destroyed but we were put here to spread our wings and fly.

Just because the devil has a plan to kill us doesn't mean that God hasn't already created a counter action plan.

We are here to let our light shine all over the world and inspire those just like us to hold on to the promise land.

How can we let someone or the devil take away our dreams and our lives that didn't give them to us? We don't even have the right to take away our own lives because we didn't give it to ourselves. So, we must push forward no matter how hard it may be or how long we go through the struggle. We can't give up on ourselves because God is going to bring us out. We can prosper and be what God wants us to be.

No matter what road you may have traveled or what road you may be on right now, you must remember that God is a forgiving God.

He will forgive you for all your sins if you just ask. He will make you the woman or man that you desire to be. I learned that through all my struggles and heart aches God never left me. I walked away from him and he waited until I returned.

Once I got back on my knees and came back to him, he was waiting for me with open arms. Love is a word that is forever searched and defined but I can truly say that I have found true Love. I am not talking about my husband, for I do love him and yes, I feel he is my soul mate. I am talking about the love that is beyond me; A love that will never hurt me no matter what; A love that will comfort me when I am confused; A love that will continue to love me until the end of time.

I am talking about, "The Love of God." For nothing can compare to it or replace it. Listen to yourself and remember that dreams do come true and you can be your greatest inspiration.

Continue to believe in yourself and never let anyone tell you, you can't do it. Never compromise you, your dreams, hopes and future for no one; for nothing can stop you if you don't allow it.

You may think you have all the time in the world but you only have one life to live.

Don't let fears hold you back from accomplishing the most important things in your life. Fear and insecurities will get you nowhere but stuck in a hole. You want to be able to feel free of all the baggage that is holding you back.

You want to be able to let go all the weights and pains that is keeping you down. Then just do it and let it go. Cut it off and move forward never looking back to return. You have the power to let go and let God. You have the power to take control of your life and circumstances and make a change.

We sometimes wonder how we could ever get up off our backs and make something happen?

Well just think about it, if we just sat around and thought about things and never put them to action then a lot of things wouldn't be.

If Martin Luther King Jr. never stood up for African American rights and what he believed in, then where would we be today? If Beethoven never believed in his heart and listened to the sound of his heart then, we would never have heard the beautiful music he created.

These two people were great people because they didn't let situations in front of them or disabilities enable them to do what they believed.

I believe that this book will inspire thousands to think about the important parts of life; to focus on their true faith and dreams; to learn to love and love to learn. I believe that this book could help millions find the love that they are looking for and avoid the things that they are not.

I believe that this book will prevent teenage pregnancy and pre-marital sex. I believe that this book will help broken marriages and broken families.

I believe that this book can bring a light to a mother or father who has no relationship with a daughter or son. I believe that this book will bring out the good in those who don't do well.

I believe that this book is more than just my road but millions of mothers, fathers, daughters or even sons have traveled. I believe that my road will lead to someone else and by me meeting that person or persons through this book, we are going to be able to change the view of the world together.

To love and live is what God created me to do. To inspire and be a light is what he told me to do. To follow his Word and share it with the world is what he commanded me to do. Now that I am listening with open ears, I can hear His voice so clearly. Until the day, I die I will do what the Lord has asked me to do, which is to, "Be Obedient."

May God be with every one that read this book and every one that didn't get to read this book but one day hears about "A Road You Must Travel".

AN ENDING TO A BEGINNING

I wanted all my life to be able to say, "My real father is a part of my life and the life of my children." I used to daydream about how he looked, smelt and felt. Did he have a look that I would instantly recognize?

Did he have a familiar smell that would jog a forgotten memory of him? Would his skin feel soft or squishy like a big teddy bear? Would I love him more the moment I lay my eyes on him or will I question all I thought I knew of him? Will I cry and hold him tight when he arrives or will I shake his hand in disbelief that he's standing in front of me? The questions kept flowing in my mind like a river of a broken dam, trying to find a place to stop.

My mind pictured that only glimpse and memory of him, at three-years-old, twenty-nine years ago. There I was standing in someone's kitchen, that was later told me was my great grandmothers' home. I stood at the kitchen screen door remembering mixed feelings of if I could trust this man that was said to be daddy. I looked up into the face of my great grandmother, a very pale skinned elderly lady.

Her skin color made me believe she was a white woman. I wasn't sure of my surroundings or myself but I listened to her words, "Don't go out child, that garage smells of feet, which is only a place for boys."

Not understanding what she meant; my little body just turned around to face the door, continuing to watch. I saw a man that I couldn't even remember if I called him daddy, jumping in this bed that was placed in the garage. My brother, who is eleven months older than I, jumped right along with him as if he was playing with his little friend.

My mother and father were married a short while and by the time I was born my mother and father had separated and decided on getting a divorce. The stories were told of how they didn't get along and the abuse that followed. My mother and father had their unhappy time, but I grew up a happy child living with my mother.

Things didn't start changing until the age of nine. I became very angry and bitter inside calling out for answers with silent facial expressions.

I didn't understand the mixed feelings of happiness and then suddenly, a sudden burst of anger, followed by sadness. I went through this stage for about a year and couldn't come to grips of what was happening in my life.

My mother didn't understand it either but questioned my sudden change in attitude. I began to feel alone inside no matter how much love and affection my mother gave me, it just wasn't enough.

I began to cling to her like a baby kangaroo to its' mothers' pouch. I began asking her questions about life and what it had to offer. I always wanted to get and understanding of the mixed feelings I had bottled inside.

It all started to come out even more when I turned ten years old. When my mind decided to choose a little boy to have my first crush on is when the desire for love became so real. The crush was like no other feelings my little heart had ever felt. My heart thumped constantly and ached at the same time for this little neighbor boy to like me. I even desired for him to love me, for in my mind I already loved him.

We had become friends through school but when we were home he was my secret boyfriend by phone. I would write in my diary how I wanted to marry him and how much I loved him.

My little crush and secret boyfriend was really all it was, a crush. He never really wanted to be my boyfriend and I came to grips that we were truly just good friends.

I still couldn't understand at that point in time in my life why I felt so strongly about this boy. I could remember crying many of nights after talking to him on the phone; sad because he wouldn't tell me he loved me. I kept asking myself, "Why did I long so much to be loved by this boy at the age of ten?" I then realized that my heart was longing for a love that this little boy couldn't give me.

I began to hold back the emotions and I questioned myself. I never seemed to get the answers that I longed for from myself.

By the time, I turned eleven years old I realized that the emptiness I felt in my heart had felt as if it turned into a hole. I felt my heart couldn't take the pain anymore and I needed help. I told my mother out of panic, that I felt something was seriously wrong with me. I told my mother I felt I had a hole in my heart, and I needed it to be fixed and fast. I felt I needed my father, and he had to be the reason for my emptiness.

My father wasn't in my life and yet he was the daddy that I needed so desperately and wanted in my life. My mother immediately said, "You don't have to be angry with your father for not being in your life because no matter what, he is still your father." I then told her that I felt I needed more love and I felt if I didn't get help soon, I would surly melt away. She then let me know that God was the only one that could fill the void that I was feeling in my heart.

The tears flowed down my face like a waterfall. I truly wanted to be fixed. I remembered all the church services I had attended. I also remembered my mother telling us that we should believe in God the Father, Jesus his son, and the Holy Spirit.

I did believe, but at this very moment I knew I had to dig just a little deeper in my belief. I had to believe that what she told me was true and put my true faith in God that he would heal me. At the age of eleven, this was my true encounter with God and his realness. I fell on my knees and my mother left the room, as to give me personal time with God. I truly wanted my hurts, pains, anger and sadness to go away.

My mother told me that for all my problems to be fixed I had to pray and believe that God can heal and fill my heart. I fell on my knees, sobbing with heartache and sincerity.

When I prayed, it felt like truly the first time I had ever uttered a word of prayer to God. With the words of meaning, I asked the Lord to be my father and take the pain I felt and make me whole. I never felt so fulfilled in my life until after I prayed that prayer. My heart never hurt like that again for the need to be loved by my father or the little boy. I in turn wanted to give love.

I asked my mother if I could contact my father for the very first time since my vague memory at the age of three. When she looked up his number, my heart raced with anticipation. When I called him, I let him know I was his little girl. I assured him that no matter what, I would call him every birthday, Christmas and Father's Day, until the day I turned eighteen. In my mind, I had planned to see him face to face by then.

The years rolled by and my promise to call continued. I always called him, no longer holding a grudge that he didn't call me. We never had real conversations; just the negative hurts he had bottled up inside of him came to surface. These were his memories of him and my mother's relationship.

Yet I seemed to feel his pain and had a little pity on him. As the years continued to go on, I began to mature. The little petty talks began to get under my skin and I no longer wanted to hear his sob stories. I heard in his voice that he wished he could tell me more than what his heart would allow, yet he just didn't know how. I knew then it was time for a change.

After six years of phone calls, he didn't allow himself to get to know his daughter. It was time for me to tell him how I felt.

A couple of months after my eighteenth birthday I prayed for a better conversation before I called him.

Yet he rambled on about what my mother did to him. I then felt it was my right and responsibility to let him know this had to stop.

I told him I no longer wanted to hear his sad song about my mother and him. I told him I no longer wanted to hear the excuses of why he wasn't a part of my life.

I no longer wanted to hear the negative vibes that flooded the phone every time we talked. I told him I would give him some time to think about what I had said and I hoped the next time we talked it would be a different song. I couldn't believe how my life jumped off and three years had passed before I picked up the phone to call him. He never tried to call me, but once again I didn't hold it against him for not doing so. Even though it had been so long, I still wanted my father to be a part of my life.

Now, I was seven and a half months pregnant with my second son and my first-born was fifteen months old. I was about to embark on a trip that I would cherish for the rest of my life.

I wrote my father a letter and surprisingly my grandfather Levi Johnson Sr. replied. I never had the opportunity to meet my grandfather.

When my grandfather replied, he told me when I was ready he would send me a two-way bus ticket so I would be able to come meet him and my father. This was a great surprise and a treat. I was so excited and overwhelmed; I couldn't wait any longer to meet these beautiful people. I wrote them back and told my grandfather I must see him and my father sooner than later.

Within three weeks I was on a Greyhound bus, with my fifteen-month-old son, and a bulging belly, excited to meet the two most important strangers in my life. It took eighteen hours to get to the beautiful city of New Orleans in the summer of 2001.

My grandfather and his wife greeted me at the bus station in the peak of darkness. They knew from the very moment I stepped off the bus I was their grandchild. I had sent them numerous pictures of the baby and me and they remembered well.

On the other hand, my grandfather and father never sent me any pictures of themselves, so I was at a guess.

The first person I remembered seeing was my grandfather, as he walked up to me holding an old wooden cane. He wore a white beard and had a round belly that outlined the frame of his body.

He seemed so fragile but sweet and smiled from ear to ear as he greeted me with a small hug. It was a bittersweet moment for we all were tired and hardly awake. I couldn't wait to see the true image of my grandfather when the sun rose later that morning.

I was anxious to see my father; the person I had waited to see for so long. When we arrived at the house, I noticed that it was just the four of us and my father wasn't there to greet me.

We all said nothing as we rushed into bed to awake to the morning sun. When morning finally had come, I was awakened to the smell of bacon, grits and eggs. My grandfathers' wife was in the kitchen making what I called, "A heavenly breakfast." She softly called me by the wrong name pronouncing it with an "r" as I sat with my son at their small round table in their small-organized kitchen.

My grandfather made his way in the kitchen with his cane in his hand to tell me what I didn't want to hear. He told me "I'm sorry but your dad is in jail but if you want to see him you can go visit him at the jail."

My heart sunk in my stomach when I received the news. I just knew that he was out all night somewhere, but jail I would have never guessed. I did feel a little upset because in my mind I had waited these years to finally meet him and he goes to jail.

"Why couldn't he have gone when I didn't make a trip to see him?" I thought to myself. I told my grandfather that jail was not the place I wanted to have a reunion, so I would just wait. I informed him that the next trip my father would have to make, to show me that he does really care. Little did I know it would take my father eight years to finally make the trip; yet when he does the time was forgotten in space.

My grandfathers' home was a small wooden white house that was maybe built in the seventy's. It had one bathroom with a little sink located in the kitchen.

The house was narrow in built and it had one bedroom just for my grandfather and his wife. The small walls of the living room space went directly to the kitchen, separated by a banister.

The bedroom followed the kitchen space and it was separated by one single door. I was so happy to be in the presence of my grandfather despite the absence of my father. My grandfather was so proud to be able to hold his first great grandson on his knee. He glowed as he went to his room to bring out all his collected pictures he had of me, my brothers and my sister.

My mother had been sending him pictures over the years to keep him informed of our location. While we went through all the old pictures and letters, it was like going into a treasure box of all the priceless treasures my grandfather had about my history.

I took everything in my heart, like the tide of the ocean on a windy day. I wanted to remember every blinking moment spent with my grandfather.

I toured through the city of New Orleans, with my brother, whom I hadn't seen in three years. My brother decided to move to New Orleans to meet our father three years prior. This was a way for him to find closure for himself.

The city it seemed was shining and full of life in the month of July. The weather was perfect and the sky seemed to smile at me with her shade of blue, sharing the space with the stratus clouds.

It seemed everything around me received my son and me, like we were a part of this atmospheric family. I spent five days and four nights getting to know the father of my father.

I felt in my heart that God sent me to spend that time with him at that very moment. I will cherish those moments for as long as I live. Unfortunately, my grandfather passed away in 2003. It took two years for me to receive the letter of notice that he had passed away.

My Aunt had written me at an old address and my neighbor was kind enough to hold on to the letter until she saw me again. I now have the peace in my heart knowing that I could spend those precious moments with him and him with his great-grandson.

Finally, the questions I had for so long were about to be answered on November 21, 2009, when my father Norwood Sr. arrived on the greyhound bus. I had it all arranged. I ordered his ticket online, makings sure he had nothing to do but show up.

He traveled eighteen hours from Baton Rouge, where he now lives, to meet my family and me. That day came faster than I realized after six months of planning and twenty-five long years of waiting; the day had finally arrived.

My husband drove while I anxiously sat in the passenger seat, while the children sat in the back seats excited to meet their grandfather for the first time. It was almost like a dream knowing that I was about to meet the man I now call pops. I never could pull the words daddy out of me but pops sounded more promising. My three boys flooded my head with questions that I didn't have the answers to about my father.

As my husband continued to drive, it felt like hours had past, even though it had only been thirty minutes.

It seemed the closer we got, the more we were blocked from getting to our destination. Cars packed the streets, while cops blocked almost every intersection, releasing the crowds from the football games held here in the City, every year.

My father now was patiently waiting for me at the station, calls to see how far away we were from picking him up. The nerves in my stomach kept building as I thought of how or if I would recognize him.

"What if he was at the wrong bus station in another city, disappointing not only me but the kids?" I questioned myself. It felt like the first day of school and I was the new student about to meet strangers for the first time. We arrived at the bus station. I walked in looking to my left and to my right for a man that I saw on a picture that had been taken over twenty-five years ago. I looked in front of me and then at the door. I knew what door he would come out of but I still didn't see anyone that resembled this picture.

I began to worry as the seconds rolled by. I carried a picture of my father when he weighed two hundred and fifty pounds, with an Afro. I didn't expect him to have an Afro now, but everything else was a thought.

My husband walked in behind me with the children and pointed out a man to my far right and said, "There's your brother's twin." It still didn't dawn on me that this man my husband was pointing at was "My Father." Then to make matters even more uncomfortable, he had been staring and smiling at me the whole time I searched for him.

I then focused my eyes on this man, who was really my father. I told myself that this was the man who helped in my creation. He weighed about one hundred and fifty pounds.

He was about five feet and nine inches, with a short haircut. He looked at me with a big smile that seemed to reach from ear to ear. When he came up to me, the thoughts rushed my mind as this stranger giggled while he greeted me.

"You look just like your mother," he giggled. Time seemed to suddenly take a shift of it's on. It felt like time froze and I was left trying to get my mind to recognize something about him. I felt I needed some type of verification that this was truly my father standing in front of me. It really was only seconds when his voice began to replay repeatedly in my head from the phone calls we had over the years.

"Yes, this is my father, my pops; yes, this is the right person." I assured myself. After picking apart his smile, his laugh and his voice; the surreal moment faded and I embraced him with two warm hugs.

I couldn't have asked for more, for he truly has a warm and open heart. He shared how he never remarried or had any more children. He says he believes it's just the way God wanted it to be.

My heart melted, as I truly began to love him even the more. He's now truly a part of my life and my family's life, holding a special place that father's hold. I enjoyed the moments we shared over a period of two weeks. He told the stories of past dramas and dramas to come.

I will never forget the laughs we shared and the good times we experienced. My father has such a big heart and I now see that he has always cared, but just needed a little help to express it.

Now we can say that we have a relationship; a relationship that will continue to grow over the years. My life has truly come into to a full circle now that I had the opportunity to meet another part of me.

This experience has placed such fulfillment in my life. The questions that I once had I now have closer.

I know now that whatever I put in my heart I can go for it. So, whatever dreams you may have or life desires, set a goal and go after it.

Don't let the world situations or other people's doubts take you from going after your hearts desires. God knows everything we seek and how to fill the voids in our lives. Even if it seems that the wait has been too long, it really hasn't. When God allows things to happen in his timing, the wait will be well worth it.

Your heart will be full and the pains will be mended. So, remember to give God all your heart and he will make all your heart desires, come to past.

MAY GOD BLESS!

The Beginning to a new end!

My Father and Me

My Husband, ("Craig",) Me and My Father

A ROAD YOU MUST TRAVEL

LATISHA FREEMAN

Made in the USA
Middletown, DE
11 March 2022

62455761R00156